THE COMPLETE MENTAL GAME OF BASEBALL

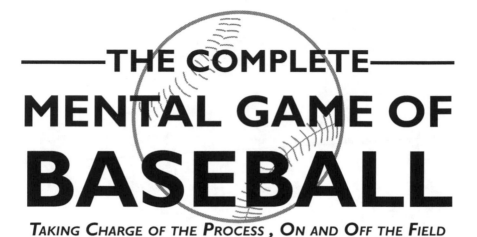

THE COMPLETE MENTAL GAME OF BASEBALL

Taking Charge of the Process, On and Off the Field

Dr. Charlie Maher

authorHOUSE®

AuthorHouse™
1663 Liberty Drive
Bloomington, IN 47403
www.authorhouse.com
Phone: 1-800-839-8640

First published by AuthorHouse 07/11/2011

ISBN: 978-1-4634-0219-8 (e)
ISBN: 978-1-4634-0220-4 (dj)
ISBN: 978-1-4634-0221-1 (sc)

Library of Congress Control Number: 2011911123

Printed in the United States of America

CONTENTS

PART THREE
COMPETITIVE FOLLOW THROUGH: BEING IN THE MOMENT

PART FOUR
ACCURATE SELF-EVALUATION: BEING REAL ABOUT RESULTS

PREFACE

This book is the result of my many years of work as a sport psychologist in major league baseball. These professional experiences have included working with players, managers, coaches, athletic trainers, and front office executives. My work has ranged from rookie ball, through all levels of the minor leagues, and up to and including the major leagues.

I am the Sport Psychologist and Director of Psychological Services for the Cleveland Indians. My role with the Indians organization spans many years, dating back to 1995. Typically, I work with the major league club and its players on their mental and emotional development, not only as performers but also as people.

I also direct the mental and emotional development of pitchers and position players in our player development (minor league) system through our mental program. In addition, I am involved in the coordination of a psychological assessment system which has been used to help make decisions about players who are eligible for the draft as well as for free agents.

RATIONALE FOR THIS BOOK

The Complete Mental Game is the name that I have given to this book since the information in the book addresses the mental and emotional needs of the baseball player, both on and off the field.

The book is an instructional system and it reflects a systematic approach to the mental side of the game.

The information in this book will guide the baseball player in learning how to use his thoughts, emotions, and actions in a number of ways: (a) to develop himself as a quality person, not only as a baseball player, (b) to cope effectively with risky people, places, and things that the player is likely to encounter during his career, (c) to be a good teammate, no matter what the player's role, and (d) to be consistent at preparing for each game, staying in the moment from pitch to pitch, and dealing constructively with results.

Through reading and then using the material in the Complete Mental Game, the baseball player will learn to take charge of the process of playing the game. By doing so, they will become their own sport psychologist and personal counselor.

When I use the term 'Complete Mental Game', I am addressing a real issue which is important to the player but that is often overlooked by players, coaches, and others. More specifically, playing the game of baseball does not occur only on the field, during actual games. Rather, a large portion of a baseball player's development and performance is influenced by what the individual does off the field—in the clubhouse, batting cages, during bullpen sessions, at school, in the home, and other places.

Playing the game of baseball, and being successful at it, is hard work. In order to be successful at playing baseball, it is best that the player have all aspects of life working for them--- not against them. In essence, the task of being a successful baseball player requires that the individual take charge of the process of playing the game, which means dealing with the important things over which they have control and influence. By taking charge of the process of playing the game and not focusing on outcomes, the player is a self-initiator, not a reactor, to their game and life. The player is involved in the Complete Mental Game.

As I have noted many times over the years when working with professional baseball players and coaches: If you want to be a quality performer on the baseball diamond, you must strive to be a quality person, off the field, since performance and person go hand in hand. The Complete Mental Game takes into account the baseball player and the person, on and off the baseball diamond, and it encourages the player to focus on the process.

During the past years, I have developed and implemented a sport psychology program within the Cleveland Indians baseball organization. It is based on this program that the Complete Mental Game has been produced.

Our evaluations of the program in the Cleveland Indians organization have indicated that the program has value for players as well as for those who coach and work with players. In this regard, there have been positive reactions to the program. Players and staff have found the program to be educational and practical. Players have learned a range of mental and emotional skills that they did not have refined before participating in the program.

Furthermore, players have been able to apply what they have learned to playing the game successfully and effectively, given their roles. Also, baseball coaches and instructional staffs have used the information in designing and implementing individual player development plans.

I believe that the time is right for me to present this program in the form of an instructional system. I have called this instructional system the Complete Mental Game, and it is covered thoroughly in this book.

WHO THIS BOOK IS FOR

The book will be useful to players, as well as to coaches and other professionals, at various levels of competitive play. This includes individuals who are involved in interscholastic competition, the collegiate ranks, as well as at the professional level, including the major leagues.

The book, however, has been directed primarily to you, the baseball player, as a resource to you so that you can proceed to be the best performer, and the best person, possible.

The content of the book will guide you in taking charge of the process of playing baseball. The process includes taking charge of how you prepare to compete, how you keep your mind in the moment from pitch to pitch, and how you deal with your results. This information will allow you to better understand yourself and to use your thoughts, emotions, and actions as you focus on the process of playing baseball.

The book provides guidelines, methods, and procedures that will allow you to learn to play the Complete Mental Game. This means that you will be ready to take charge of your personal process, and to enable you to be the best that you can be, at four levels of psychological development.

The four levels of your psychological development are:
(1) *The Person:* You will learn about developing a perspective that allows you to balance baseball effectively with the rest of your life. You will learn how to make sure that you have

an accurate understanding of yourself as a person. This includes knowing your personality; being able to clarify your core values; and determining how to best relate to other people including players, coaches, and umpires. To get the most from developing and fine tuning yourself as a person, you will be guided in taking the time to understand your strengths and limitations and how to firm up personal commitments.

(II) *The "Coper":* You will learn how to strengthen specific mental and emotional skills so that you can cope effectively with the risks that you are likely to encounter in and around the baseball environment. Through perspective taking, personal awareness, and mental discipline, you will learn how to avoid risky people, places, and things, all of which can derail you and your baseball career. Being an effective "coper" allows you to stay away from gamblers and other people who want to drag you down; enables you to avoid bars and clubs; and helps you to not abuse drugs, alcohol, and performance enhancing substances. You can be ready to weed out negative influences on your life and your game, while building a positive support system of family and friends.

(III) *The Teammate:* You will learn to challenge yourself to be a good teammate. Being a good teammate starts with your readiness and willingness to commit to something larger than you—that is, to the team. Learning how you can balance your own needs as a baseball player with those of the team and your role on the team will give you a leg up on how others perceive and evaluate you, including individuals like coaches, scouts, and your teammates. Being a good teammate also frees you up to be a valuable contributor to the team, including becoming a leader in the clubhouse and on the field.

(IV) *The Performer:* This level can be considered as the "bottom line" of baseball in that it deals with playing the game and focusing on the process of playing the game, one pitch at a time. However, it builds on the other three levels. As you will learn, performing to your best on any given day, however, is enhanced by adhering to three core mental principles. These are: (1) Being ready to compete (*Quality Preparation*); (2) Being actively and productively engaged in the game (*Competitive Follow Through*): and (3) Dealing constructively with your results (*Accurate Self-Evaluation*).

The book is written for any player—you included—who wants to learn about the mental side of baseball in a complete way, and who wants to be their best, on and off the baseball diamond.

In addition, baseball coaches will find the book useful, especially for implementing a mental program with their teams.

Likewise, the book will be informative to other individuals and groups including sport psychologists and mental skills consultants, and it also has value for parents and spouses of players.

How the Book is Organized

The book is organized around four major parts. Each part includes several chapters. Each one of these chapters will provide you with practical information about the various aspects of the Complete Mental Game. Overall, there are 16 chapters in the book. There also are several appendices to the book.

In essence, each chapter of the book can be considered as a mini-book, or manual, and it can be read independently of the other chapters. However, it is recommended that all of the chapters of the book be read first in sequence in order to get the most out of the material. Then, you can go back to individual chapters, and study specific chapters, based on your needs.

The first part of the book is entitled '*The Foundation: Being Well Grounded*'. In this section, there are four chapters. These chapters form the underlying basis—or the foundation—for the Complete Mental Game.

The chapters in this part will provide you with information about the following topics:

Chapter 1—*The Three Sides of Baseball*—You will become acquainted with the three sides of the game of baseball--- the physical, mental, and fundamental sides. You will learn how each side of the game depends on the other two sides and how the mental side, which is the focus of this book, contributes to the physical and fundamental sides.

Chapter 2—*Thoughts, Emotions, and Actions*—Your thoughts, emotions and actions, and how you use them, influence the mental side of your game. Thoughts, emotions, and actions are the assets which you have to work with as a performer and as a person. If you use them correctly, they can work in your favor as a baseball player and person.

Chapter 3—*The Process of Playing the Game*—In this chapter, you will be provided an overview about the process of playing the game. The process of playing the game involves preparing for and being engaged in the game; being able and willing to pay attention to things over which you have control; and letting go of your results. The process includes using your thoughts, emotions, and actions in preparing for each game; in keeping your mind in the moment one pitch at a time; and in evaluating your performance accurately.

Chapter 4—*The Complete Mental Game Blueprint*—In this chapter, you will be given a blueprint for learning to play the Complete Mental Game. This chapter will allow you to conduct an assessment of yourself on a range of mental domains. In this regard, you will learn how you can use the blueprint for your continued development and success as a baseball player.

The second part, *Quality Preparation: Being Ready to Compete*, is centered on the first core mental principle. In this section, there also are four chapters. Each chapter will provide you with information about how to get yourself ready to compete, mentally and emotionally, not only for each game but also over the longer haul of the season and throughout your career in baseball.

Each chapter describes a particular mental domain, provides guidelines for how you can develop and improve yourself in the domain, and concludes with mental exercises.

Chapter 5—*Perspective*—This chapter will address the mental domain which has to do with balancing baseball with the rest of your life. This chapter will include procedures for the important mental skill of values clarification and other mental skills, such as charting a vision for success.

Chapter 6—*Personal Awareness*—In this chapter, you will learn how to pinpoint your current strong points and limitations as a baseball player and how to use that information for your overall development as a player and as a person.

Chapter 7—*Self-Motivation*—This chapter is devoted to guiding you to set goals, which are SMART—Specific, Measureable, Attainable, Relevant, and Time Framed. Your attention to and enthusiastic pursuit of these kind of goals will help make you a better player and prevent you from setting vague goals as well as goals that can distract you and limit your development and performance.

Chapter 8—*Mental Discipline*—This chapter focuses on what it means to you to have a plan and how to follow through with it. In this chapter, you learn about the different type of plans, including pre game routines and game plans, and how to use them to your competitive advantage.

The third part, *Competitive Follow Through: Being in the Moment*, addresses the second core mental principle. The five chapters in this part of the book will provide you with information about how to effectively compete, not only as the baseball game begins but also how to sustain your competitiveness throughout the contest. Each chapter includes a description of a mental domain, instructional guidelines and mental exercises.

The chapters in this part address the following content:

Chapter 9—*Self-Confidence*—In this chapter, you will learn about believing in your capacity to compete, one pitch at a time, during game competition. The task of developing and maintaining confidence is not easy, nor is it easily sustained.

However, there are proven ways to keep your confidence up and to get it back when you lose it.

Chapter 10—*Emotional Intensity*—Competing at an effective level of energy and effort throughout the game is important to your success no matter what your position. In this chapter, you will be guided in how to gauge your intensity level and how to effectively make adjustments in it as the game proceeds.

Chapter 11—*Focus*—In this chapter, you will learn how to keep your mind in the moment, how to accept what is given to you, and how to pay attention to what really matters, pitch to pitch.

Chapter 12—*Composure*—This chapter considers how you can become skilled at remaining poised under competitive pressure. This includes being able to step back, breathe deeply, relax, and not judge yourself.

Chapter 13—*Teamwork*—Teamwork is a mental domain that has to do with how you relate productively to teammates, coaches, and others. In this chapter, you will learn how ready you are to buy into something which is larger than yourself and how to make personal adjustments so that you can be a good teammate.

The fourth and concluding part, *Accurate Self-Evaluation: Being Real about Results,* will discuss the third core mental principle. In this part, there are three chapters. Each chapter will provide you with information about how to be honest and objective with your performance and how to use that information to make effective adjustments. These chapters include:

Chapter 14—*Self-Esteem*—This chapter involves learning about being a good separator of who you are as a performer and as a person. It involves learning to keep yourself on an even keel, no matter how you perform, inning by inning, pitch by pitch.

Chapter 15—*Performance Accountability*—In this chapter, you will learn about taking responsibility for your results and in using performance information for making adjustments to how you play the game, given your position.

Chapter 16—*Continuous Improvement*—Striving to make adjustments to your game and to your life is the focus of this chapter. How you can develop a procedure for your continuous education and lifelong learning also will be covered.

REMINDER AND BEST WISHES

Please take note here: this book is not entertainment. Rather, the book is an instructional system. It is best read with mental discipline and only when you are ready and willing to devote real time to your mental game and its development and improvement.

If you want to be the best that you can be as a baseball player and person, then you must devote quality time to the mental side of the game. If so, the material in this book will give you a framework and tools to do the job—to play the Complete Mental Game.

This book is not a collection of stories about baseball players, nor is it pop psychology. Everything contained in the chapters of the book has been applied successfully by professional baseball players and players at collegiate and lower levels.

I hope that you find this book as a valuable resource to guide your own mental and emotional development as a baseball player and as a person.

ACKNOWLEDGEMENTS

I thank all of the Cleveland Indians players and the other professional baseball players who have participated with me over the years in the development and use of the instructional system and the material which is contained in this book. In particular, I acknowledge Mark Shapiro, General Manager of the Cleveland Indians, who has provided me with unswerving support and opportunities to design and implement a sport psychology program in the Indians organization. I also appreciate the efforts of the range of managers and coaches who have been part of this process, especially Eric Wedge. Finally, I have been fortunate to have had the assistance of Jennifer Gibson in the preparation of the manuscript for this book.

PART ONE

THE FOUNDATION: BEING WELL GROUNDED

CHAPTER ONE

──────── ⚾ ────────

THE THREE SIDES OF BASEBALL

There are three sides to the game of baseball. They are the physical side, the fundamental side, and the mental side. The physical side has to do with your physical condition. The fundamental side involves your baseball skills. The mental side covers your thoughts, emotions, and actions.

The three sides of the game—physical, mental, and fundamental—all are relevant to your development, performance, and success as a baseball player. If you expect to be a good baseball player, or a great one, you cannot neglect any of the three sides of baseball.

How good you are at each side of baseball contributes to your overall game. This is the case no matter who you are or whether you are a pitcher or a position player. It does not matter if you are a starter, role player, or a utility specialist.

Your understanding and appreciation of the three sides of the game also applies to you, no matter what your current level of competitive play—high school, college, or professional—and no matter the win- loss record of your team, or the time of the year.

If you want to be the best baseball player possible, all three sides of the game must be taken into account by you, the baseball player. The three sides of baseball to which I am referring are:

1. *Physical Side*: This side includes your core muscular strength, flexibility, quickness, cardiovascular fitness, nutrition, and other physical areas.

2. *Fundamental Side*: This side has to do with the specific

baseball skills that you need to possess in order to be effective in your role and position. The fundamental side includes skill areas involved with hitting, fielding, throwing, base running, catching, and pitching.

3. *Mental Side*: This is the side that has to do with your thoughts, emotions, and actions and how you use them, both on the baseball diamond and off of it. This side of the game is what this book is about and it is being referred in this book as the Complete Mental Game.

These three sides of the game of baseball are illustrated by the equal-sided triangle, seen as Figure 1.1.

Figure 1.1: The Three Sides of the Game of Baseball

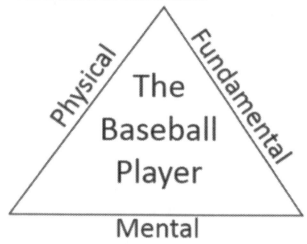

Each of these three sides of baseball is important to your development, performance, and success as a baseball player.

Interactions of the Three Sides of the Game

The three sides of the game of baseball interact with one another in many important ways. These interactions have an effect on you and how you play the game.

Just how you go about developing and improving yourself in relation to one side of the game will affect the other two sides, either for the better or in ways that can limit your performance.

For example, consider the baseball player who is sound in terms of the fundamental side of the game. This player possesses good fundamentals for his position and consistently demonstrates these fundamentals on the field. He is solid in his approach to hitting and he is able to field his position, say third base.

However, if this player is not physically in condition to play a full game at third base, or if he is too tired to put up quality at bats, or to field his position, then both the fundamental side of his game and the mental side of his game are likely to be affected, probably for the worst, thereby limiting the player's performance.

Because this baseball player is not in good physical shape, he will not have the stamina to compete effectively throughout the contest, inning to inning. As the game proceeds, his hitting and his third base play, although sound fundamentally, may likely become less efficient and become more inconsistent, due to physical and mental fatigue.

In contrast, consider the starting pitcher who is physically in very good condition. If his fundamental side is not sufficiently developed, however, like if he does not have command of his pitches due to poor delivery mechanics, then this pitcher's overall performance probably will be inconsistent. Or, if this pitcher is not in control of his emotions, then his delivery may very likely be rushed, resulting in lack of command of his pitches.

As another example: If a position player, or a pitcher, has not developed the mental side of his game—which is the focus of this book—the physical and fundamental aspects of the player's game also will be negatively affected.

On the other hand, though, if a baseball player takes into account all three sides of the game—the physical, fundamental, and mental—and works at developing them all, then this individual's overall progress as a player and his day to day performance will most likely be enhanced.

More often than not, the player who addresses all three sides of the game will continue to get closer to realizing his potential as a baseball player. This will be the case since all three sides are being developed and working in coordination with one another.

PREVENT THE SHORTCHANGING OF YOUR DEVELOPMENT

In the Complete Mental Game, there is clear recognition that all three sides of the game—the physical, mental, and fundamental—are equally important. This means that all three sides require your continued attention, practice, monitoring, and adjustment.

This kind of personal attention on your part is never ending and this is the case whether you are a high school player, a college competitor, or a major leaguer.

In essence, you cannot shortchange yourself in any of the three sides of the game. One side of the game is not better than the other. Instead, all sides are important; all deserve appropriate attention, time, and effort.

The individual who plays the Complete Mental Game embraces all three sides of the game of baseball and strives to be the best that he can be in each area.

Table 1.1 summarizes essential areas which comprise each side of the game of baseball.

The rest of this current chapter will briefly review some basic areas and qualities for each side of the game.

The remaining chapters of the book, then, will cover in detail the mental side of the game.

TABLE 1.1. Three sides of the game of baseball: Basic Areas

Side	Area
Physical	• Core strength, flexibility • Cardio fitness, quickness • Diet, nutrition, vision
Fundamental	• Hitting, fielding, throwing • Running, catching, pitching
Mental	• Thoughts, emotions, actions • Preparation, competitiveness • Self-evaluation

THE PHYSICAL SIDE

The physical side of baseball has to do with your natural athleticism and other physical characteristics.

Without doubt, your muscles and their muscular strength are important to how you perform. Likewise, your heart and its cardio vascular functioning are essential aspects of your physical development.

In addition to muscular strength, the flexibility of your joints, and your physical quickness, particularly first step quickness, are necessary for success in baseball.

Other dimensions of the physical side which are important to a baseball player include vision, diet, nutrition, the neurological area, and overall general health.

In terms of the development of the physical side of your game, you need to make the mental and emotional commitment to make sure that your physical strength and condition are the best that they can be.

In order to make sure that physical side of the game has an important place, all professional baseball organizations, most college baseball programs, and an increasing number of high school programs have strength and conditioning coaches as part of their staffs.

Many of these programs also have added a nutritional consultant as part of their support services to their player.

THE FUNDAMENTAL SIDE

The fundamental side of the game of baseball is, of course, where most of the attention is given to the player and his development.

This attention is natural and warranted since, without an appropriate level of fundamental skills, it will be difficult for any player to be competitive on a consistent basis and not overmatched.

The fundamental side of the game is basic to success on the field. In this regard, you are encouraged to make sure that you are developing and applying the proper mechanics and skills for playing the game, both offensively and defensively.

The fundamental side of the game can be divided into a number of important skill areas, referred to as baseball skills.

For position players, these baseball skill areas encompass hitting, bunting, fielding, base running and base stealing.

For pitchers, sound delivery mechanics can be considered as a basic fundamental skill. In addition, pitchers need to be skilled at other things particularly fielding their position and controlling the running game.

In terms of the development of your fundamental baseball skills—no matter what your position—you also need to be able to adopt a listen and learn attitude.

The kind of commitment that you need to make to the successful development of the fundamental side of your game requires a willingness on your part to want to strive to get better and to never take anything for granted.

As a baseball player gets older and matures both physically and mentally, some fundamental skill areas will decline. As a result, other baseball skills will need to take precedence. This progression and decline will occur as part of your game, if it already has not happened yet.

The baseball player must be ready, willing, and able to change in the fundamental side of the game, to make continuous improvements and adjustments.

THE MENTAL SIDE

The mental side of the game, of course, is the focus of this book. The remaining chapters will be devoted to all aspects of the mental side of the game.

In and of itself, the mental side of baseball can also be represented as a triangle, also with three equal sides.

The three sides of the mental part of the game have to do with three basic ingredients. These are your thoughts, emotions, and actions. These are three of your most important assets as a baseball player and as a person.

One of the great things about the mental side of baseball is that you are able to influence and use your thoughts, emotions, and actions to your competitive advantage…if you want to and know how.

Taking charge of the process of playing baseball involves taking charge of your thoughts, emotions, and actions. This book is about how to take charge of the process.

The diagram representing the basic ingredients of the mental side of the game of baseball is seen as Figure 1.2

The three aspects of the mental side of baseball are your thoughts, emotions, and actions. How you use your thoughts, emotions, and actions will, in large part, determine how you will function, both on and off the baseball diamond.

Your *thoughts* are the vision, images, and words that you produce while preparing for competition. Your thoughts have a lot to do with the quality of how you are actually engaged in playing the game, and at other times in your life off the field.

Some of the thoughts that you experience are helpful to you and are considered positive thoughts. For example, thinking that you have prepared well for an upcoming game and that you are ready to compete from the first pitch on will help to give you confidence and focus.

Figure 1.2: Basic ingredients of the complete mental game of baseball.

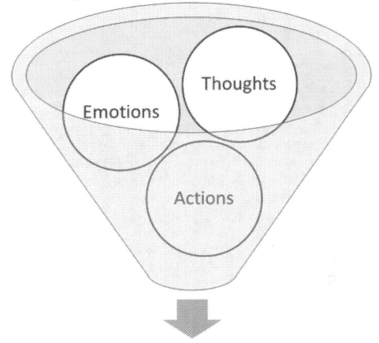

The Complete Mental Game
On the field, Off the field

Other thoughts, however, can serve to limit your performance and these are negative or self-defeating thoughts. Examples of negative thinking are thoughts such as worrying about getting out of the inning rather than focusing on the upcoming pitch. Negative thoughts can undermine the performance of a pitcher, or a position player, very easily and quickly at that.

In addition, the quality of the thoughts which a baseball player has affects how he reasons while he is competing, as well as how he goes about solving problems and making decisions, off the baseball diamond. When the player's thoughts are objective and not unduly influenced by emotions, the player's decision making is likely to be clear and effective, more often than not.

Your *emotions* have to do with the things that you are sensing and feeling, before, during, and after the game. Emotions include what you are experiencing, both on and off the field. In this regard, your emotions may be described as being positive or negative and productive or unproductive in terms of your performance.

Examples of positive emotions that affect you, the baseball player, are your passion for playing the game, joy about winning a close game, and appreciation for working hard and making the team.

Examples of negative emotions which can affect your play are becoming angry at striking out as part of an at-bat, frustration when not getting hitters out as a pitcher, and jealousy when a teammate gets attention from others such as the media.

Your *actions* reflect behaviors such as implementing a pre-game routine, following through on your plan for an at-bat, staying away from bars, clubs, and people who do not have your best intentions at heart, and saying no to drugs of abuse and other banned substances.

Thoughts, emotions, and actions affect and influence how the baseball player, including you, prepares, competes, and evaluates his performance. They are basic ingredients of the mental side of the game.

The Complete Mental Game is based on recognition that your thoughts, emotions, and actions are very important personal assets. They can be developed, refined, and improved, day in and day out, both on and off the baseball diamond. You have the responsibility to make your thoughts, emotions, and actions work for you.

EXERCISES

1. What does the game of baseball mean to you? What attracted you to the game? Why do you persist in playing it?

2. If the game of baseball ended tomorrow—that is, there was no more sport of baseball—what would you do with the time that you devote to the game?

3. How would you size up your physical development? How much time do you spend on it? What has deterred you from getting better physically?

4. What about the fundamental side of your game? What are you

satisfied with in terms of your fundamental development? What are you less than satisfied with? What are your intentions in terms of your fundamental development and improvement?

5. How much time have you spent on the mental side of your game? Who has been helpful to you in its development? How much time do you think that you should put into your mental development?

6. What would you like to learn more about in terms of the mental side of the game?

7. How would you describe yourself at this time as a baseball player? How would you like to describe yourself as a baseball player in a few years? At the conclusion of your baseball career?

CHAPTER TWO

———— ⬤ ————

THOUGHTS, EMOTIONS, AND ACTIONS

Baseball is not an easy game to play, at any level. In baseball, you will fail more than you will succeed. Making solid contact with the ball with two men on base and two outs, for example, takes confidence, focus, and a disciplined approach. Likewise, throwing a change up in a three and two count requires composure. Turning a double play is not a walk in the park, especially when a runner is heading right into you.

The game of baseball is hard and demanding. To have success as a baseball player requires development in the three sides of the game—top physical condition, solid fundamentals, and effective mental skills.

Despite the difficulties involved in playing baseball, the game can be an enjoyable experience, especially when you develop and use all of the assets which are at your beck and call.

With respect to the Complete Mental Game, there are three important personal assets that you can take advantage of—leverage to your benefit—if you want to be deal successfully with the ups and downs of the game, its success and failures.

The three personal assets that you have at your disposal as a baseball player, and as a person who plays baseball, are the following:

1. Your *thoughts*—the images, words, and ideas that you think about and tell yourself about, both on and off the field.

2. Your *emotions*—the effort and energy that you sense and feel when you are playing baseball as well as at other times and in other places, off the field.

3.   Your *actions*—the behaviors, steps, and activities that you display and follow through on, as a player and as a person.

Without a doubt, how you think about yourself as a player and person; how you use your emotions on and off the field; and how you behave in the clubhouse and in other areas of your life can help make or break your performance, and your career, in baseball.

Figure 2.1 shows the relationship between your thoughts, emotions, and actions as a baseball player.

Figure 2.1: Relationships of thoughts, emotions, and actions as a baseball player.

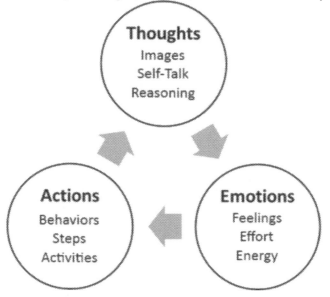

INVESTING IN YOUR THOUGHTS, EMOTIONS, AND ACTIONS

To be the best baseball player that you can be, it is in your best interest to invest in the three personal assets—your thoughts, emotions, and actions.

Investing in your thoughts, emotions, and actions means developing and using these personal assets in the following ways:

1.   Developing and using your thoughts, emotions, and actions so that you can be a *quality person*. This includes understanding your personality, clarifying your core personal values, and being aware of cultural similarities and differences that you share with teammates and opponents.

2. Developing and using your thoughts, emotions, and actions so that you can effectively *cope with risk*. This includes eliminating negative people, places, and things from your life while building a positive support system of family and friends.

3. Developing and using your thoughts, emotions, and actions so that you can be a *good teammate*. This allows you to contribute to the team, no matter what your role on the team may be, as well as stepping up and being a team leader when appropriate.

4. Developing and using your thoughts, emotions, and actions so that you can be a *consistent performer*. This includes having a systematic way of preparing for the game, being able to stay in the moment and compete pitch to pitch, and dealing with results and making adjustments.

Four Levels of Psychological Development

There are four psychological levels at which you can develop and use your thoughts, emotions, and actions. Figure 2.2 is a visual illustration of these four levels.

Figure 2.2: Four levels of psychological development of the baseball player.

Level One: The Player as a Person

At this first level of psychological development, your main consideration is using your thoughts, emotions, and actions to understand who you are as a person, what your core values are, and other areas.

If you spend time in getting to know yourself as a person, and make needed changes in how you approach things, you will set a solid foundation for positive development at the other three levels.

In order to develop yourself as a quality person—which is the bottom rung of the pyramid in Figure 2.2—you must be willing to commit to understanding yourself and becoming more aware of who you are as a person. This is referred to as your personality.

PERSONALITY

Your personality consists of the basic human traits which define you and make you up as a person. Your personality includes your predominant thoughts, emotions, and actions

Increasingly, professional baseball organizations are assessing the personality of their draft and free agent prospects. As part of the Cleveland Indians, we have conducted personality assessments not only of draft prospects but also of our players. We have done this because of the premium we have placed on understanding and assisting the player as a person.

What are these basic areas of your personality that have relevance to you as a baseball player and as a person?

Five basic personality traits which are important for baseball players are the following:

1. *Relationships with Others*—This trait has to do with how you interact with other people, particularly with teammates and coaches. Are you open and outgoing, or quiet and reserved? Do you listen to others? Are you considered as being coachable? Are you flexible in how you relate to individuals, depending whether you are on the field, in the clubhouse, or during team travel?

2. *Coping with Stressors*—This trait involves how you cope with worry and doubt and deal with things when the outcomes are not clear, especially when they are not within your control. Are you low in anxiety or high in anxiety? Are you tense and very hard on yourself? Do you tend to deny things? Do you tend to deal with stress in self-destructive ways (e.g., drugs and alcohol)?

3. *Personal Problem Solving*—This trait reflects how you approach problems and tasks in everyday life. Are you objective and unemotional in solving problems? Or, do you become overly emotional and not sufficiently objective and let your emotions get in the way?

4. *Independence*—This represents how you go about completing day to day tasks and workouts, such as batting practice and bullpen sessions, especially when you are left on your own.

Do you wait for others such as your coaches to take the initiative or do you start things on your own? Do you tend to rush or cut corners?

5. *Self Control*—This trait is about how you manage your impulses to act. Are you thoughtful and reflective? Or, are you quick to act and impulsive?

CORE VALUES

In baseball as well as in other sports, the word, character, has become a frequently used term.

Front office executives, scouts, managers, and coaches all want to know what kind of person the organization is getting, if they draft any particular player.

In essence, your character can be described by what you value in life, especially your core personal values.

Your core personal values are the things that have meaning for you and which are over and above baseball. Core personal values are things in your life that are most important to you. Core values may include things like staying healthy, having a good family life, helping other people who are less fortunate, and other things of value.

Defining your core values is a worthwhile use of your thoughts, emotions, and actions. It involves thinking about and answering these questions

1. What do I care about in my life?

2. What gives meaning to my existence?

3. What makes me a quality individual?

4. What do I really want that has merit for me and others?

CULTURAL AWARENESS AND SENSITIVITY

Without doubt, baseball is an international sport. Given the diversity of baseball and its international thrusts, you are encouraged to use your thoughts, emotions, and actions so that you respect, and appreciate the diversity of cultures of the players who are your teammates and those whom you compete against.

This could mean actions such as learning to become conversant in another language such as Spanish in order to better relate to some of your teammates.

It might mean becoming familiar with the food and family customs of your teammates. It may have to do with developing an appreciation of how players from other cultures prepare for games. It could mean asking a player from another culture to dinner.

Level Two: The Player as a "Coper"

No matter what the level of competition or league in which you find yourself, when you play baseball you are in a high risk environment. Travel, hotels, unfamiliar locations, practices, and being around a range of people, among other factors, are part and parcel of the game.

However, these factors can also place you at risk for going in the wrong direction and against your core values, if you are not a good "coper", someone who can deal with risk and effectively manage it. This is the case particularly at the professional level and collegiate level, but increasingly so in high schools. Risk and the game are often inseparable.

There are many kinds of risks which you can encounter as a baseball player.

1. One type of risk is that of *physical risk*. By not having a plan for injury prevention, you may be putting yourself at risk for shoulder, arm and leg problems, torn tendons, or strained ligaments, among other things.

2. Another type of risk has to do with *financial risk*. If you have a college scholarship or a professional baseball contract in hand, you can lose the funds quickly if you don't know how to handle them. How do you plan to manage your money wisely and effectively? What kind of financial advice are you receiving?

3. Another kind of risk involves two parts: *mental risk* and *emotional risk*. Mental risk occurs when you think before you act putting yourself in jeopardy. In addition, emotional risk refers to being impatient, greedy, and selfish.

What will help you to cope effectively with mental and emotional risk is how skilled you are at handling People, Places, and Things—your PPTs.

Some PPTs are self-destructive or negative and they can derail your career. In contrast, other PPTs are supportive and positive and can enhance your career and propel it on a positive path. Your task is to lock into the positive PPTs and eliminate the negative PPTs.

PEOPLE

Negative people are individuals who can get you in trouble, both on and off the baseball diamond. Negative people include any individual or group of individuals which can pull you in the wrong direction and limit your baseball career.

These individuals and groups could be anywhere and come from anywhere and come on the scene at any time. They could be classmates, friends from your home town, someone seeking to sell you something, or any other person who does not have your best interests at heart.

In contrast, there are people who are your supporters and who you trust. They also can include family, classmates, teammates, coaches and others. These people are the ones who constitute your personal support system.

PLACES

Some facilities and locations also can place you at risk, both mentally and emotionally.

These negative places or locations can be anywhere. Typically, they include bars, clubs, dormitory rooms, hotel rooms, wherever risky living may be going on.

In contrast, there are positive places to which you can find refuge including your place of residence, the clubhouse, and other locations that are aligned with your core values.

THINGS

Self-destructive things refer primarily to substances which, if ingested, can hurt your game and, if used on a regular basis or abused, can derail your baseball career.

Here, I am referring to things like drugs of abuse, such as marijuana and cocaine, performance enhancing substances such as steroids and amphetamines, and a range of nutritional supplements. Positive things include a sound diet and nutritional foods.

Are you up to the challenge of coping effectively with the PPTs in your life, so that you can minimize mental and emotional risk?

I will provide guidelines for dealing with people, places, and things in the book. This will occur especially in the chapters dealing with mental discipline, composure, and self-esteem.

LEVEL THREE: THE PLAYER AS A TEAMMATE

Baseball is a team game. As a team game, you have teammates; you are part of something larger than yourself. Some of these teammates are more closely aligned with the team and its goals. These are typically solid members of the team.

There also may be individuals who are on the roster and also are a part of the team. However, they have not bought into the team approach, at least not in a full way.

Players who are good teammates contribute to the team. No matter what their role, these players identify with the team and are members of it.

Players who are not good teammates leave something to be desired. They are not members of the team but just occupy a spot on it. They have difficulty buying into collective goals. Their focus is on themselves. They can be considered as selfish.

For your own career, it is better for you to be a good teammate, rather than one who is considered as a poor one. Your reputation in the game and the evaluations that other people make of you as a teammate, including scouts, rest on how you come across as a teammate.

In order to judge yourself on how you stack up as a teammate, consider the following factors that have to do with being a good teammate:

COMMITMENT TO TEAM PURPOSE

This involves your willingness to acknowledge some things which are larger than yourself—these are the team and its goals.

The commitment to team purpose also is reflected by the actions which you take as a teammate. Are these actions in accord with the team and its purpose? To what extent are you recognized as being a contributor to the team by players, coaches, and staff?

Another important indicator is your willingness as a player to make changes in your role on the team.

Desire for Team Membership

In this area, you are being sized up for how you are as a contributor to the team, an integral part of it.

This task involves your personal identification with the team and how you are perceived. Are you seen as a member of the team or just tying up a roster spot on it?

The team member is enthused when the team wins, even if he did not have a chance to contribute to the win.

Interpersonal Relations with Players, Coaches, and Staff

In this area, the valuable teammate is a good listener. You pay attention to what is being said and ask questions as appropriate. Furthermore, you assist other players with learning the game.

When differences of opinion arise or when there is a conflict situation, you are able to resolve it in ways that respect others and that respect the game.

In the second part of the book, there will be an entire chapter devoted to teamwork.

Level Four: The Player as a Performer

Playing baseball and performing as expected is what the game is about, for the large part. This is why most individuals want to play the game.

Performance, as we will be discussing it as part of the Complete Mental Game, has to do with accomplishments.

Performance accomplishments are things like putting the ball in play, moving the runner with a bunt, getting the ball to the right cutoff man at the right time, keeping the ball down. Performance accomplishments add value to your game and to your team.

As we are using the term, performance does not have to do with your numbers, game statistics. If you are a good performer, you are doing the little things effectively and you are playing the game the right way.

Being a good performer builds on the other psychological levels already discussed—Levels I, II, III.

If you are a solid person, take the time to plan for and minimize risk, and become a team member, you are likely going to be good performer, if you work at it.

Effective performance is correlated with things that happen before, during, and after the game.

These things involve your thoughts, emotions, and actions.

Effective performance is seen in how you prepare for each game, how you compete pitch to pitch during the contest, and how you deal with your results including making adjustments.

How good a performer are you? Here are some things which fall in this area:

PREPARATION

1. How do I get myself mentally and emotionally ready to compete?

2. How much value do I place on my preparation and its quality?

COMPETITIVENESS

3. How do I go about competing from pitch to pitch?

4. How do I sustain my competitiveness inning to inning and throughout the contest?

SELF-EVALUATION

5. How do I react to my results?

6. How do I use feedback about my performance to improve myself?

Performance will be the center of attention in most of the remaining chapters of the book.

EXERCISES

1. During the past six months or so, what has been something that you have been very proud of as a person, over and above baseball? Why have you been proud of this?

2. During the past twelve months, what is something you have done as a person, outside of the game, that you wished that you could have back and do again?

3. What are people, places, and things that, if you do not watch out for, could sidetrack you and your baseball career?

4. How would your teammates describe you, if they were asked to write something about you as a teammate?

5. As a performer, what can you be counted on to do? What is an area of your performance that you sometimes neglect to pay attention to?

6. What would you like to learn more about in terms of understanding your thoughts, emotions, and actions on and off the baseball diamond? Why?

CHAPTER THREE

THE PROCESS OF PLAYING THE GAME

A baseball player's ability to take charge of the process of playing baseball is a basic foundation for his success in the game. The process of playing the game of baseball is seen in how the player is involved with the factors that are under his control and influence, both on and off the field.

By taking charge of the process of playing the game—how you prepare, compete, react to results, and make adjustments—you give yourself a good chance to play the game the right way.

By taking charge of the process, you have decided to deal with the factors that are within your control and influence. As already discussed in Chapter 2, these controllable factors include your most important personal assets: your thoughts, emotions, and actions.

The process of playing the game is about being ready, willing, and able to use your personal assets—thoughts, emotions, and actions—so that you can prepare, compete, deal with results and make adjustments.

In terms of the process of playing the game, your thoughts, emotions and actions determine how you proceed with the following:

1. How you prepare yourself to compete for each game (*Quality Preparation*).

2. How you compete, pitch by pitch, at the beginning of the game and throughout it (*Competitive Follow Through*).

3. How you react to your results once the game is over but before the next one (*Accurate Self-Evaluation*).

The process of playing the game is not about baseball outcomes. In this regard, outcomes like getting hits, or reaching a certain level of statistical performance, are not within your control. Too many factors when playing the game can work against you as to whether you get a hit, or whether you give up an earned run, among other things.

Taking charge of the process of playing the game, however, is something that you can focus on and that you can have work for you. Focusing on the process means dealing with things which you can influence and control. In essence, these are your personal assets—your thoughts, emotions, and actions.

If you take charge and create a good process for yourself, and if you stay focused on it, then your outcomes and results will take care of themselves. Since you cannot control outcomes, but you can control the process, it makes sense for you to take charge of and to focus on the process.

More basically, taking charge of the process of playing the game means taking charge of your thoughts, emotions, and actions.

If a baseball player consistently embraces the process of playing the game, and if that individual can be comfortable with a process focus rather than an outcomes focus, then positive outcomes are more likely to result for him and his team.

In contrast, if the player wants to focus on his numbers and outcomes, and not make the process a priority, then positive outcomes are likely to be less than expected.

Focusing on the process of playing baseball is a mindset, a mental and emotional experience, and a series of steps and activities. A few examples follow.

When a starting pitcher decides to use the five days between his outings in a focused and systematic way to get ready to pitch, then he is taking charge of the process. This pitcher's process starts with establishing a five day routine that gets him ready to compete when he gets the ball every fifth day and then following through with that routine, day by day.

The pitcher's five day routine is likely to include physical activities like running; some work in the weight room; review of video tape of his last performance and upcoming opponent; and bullpen sessions with the pitching coach, among other things. If the pitcher maps out and commits to this five day routine, he is taking charge of the process of his preparation.

When a position player commits to having quality at bats, he can take charge of the process of competing, to his advantage. For example, this committed player can develop a process for his at-bats. This process may include implementing a pre-game routine, one which includes a plan for how he approaches his at bats, coupled with work off the batting tee, and taking batting practice. Then, he can follow the process which he has established for each game. All of this reflects the process of playing the game.

In addition, when a player spends time reviewing his game performance following the game, first alone and then with a coach, he is also involved in the process of evaluating his performance.

Furthermore, when a player decides how to avoid bars and clubs so that these things do not derail his season and career, he is dealing with the process of coping with risk. When the player plans a healthy diet and gets a good night's sleep before coming to the ballpark, he also is taking charge of the process of being physically ready to perform.

WHERE DOES THE PROCESS FIT IN?

A process is something that is planned, fluid, and systematic. If the process is followed by the baseball player, he will be setting the conditions for himself so that he can get desired results, more often than not.

A process is the way in which any performer, including a baseball player, goes about doing things (process), in order to accomplish things (outcomes). Most performers in any sport or in any walk of life rely on effective processes.

The essence of the process of playing the game of baseball is seen visually in Figure 3.1.

Figure 3.1: The process of playing the game of baseball.

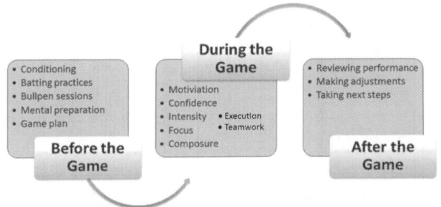

This figure shows that there are three separate, yet interrelated time frames which form the process of playing the game of baseball. These time frames of the process of playing the game of baseball are the following:

1. *Before the Game*—This is the time when the player gets prepared to play the game. This time period typically involves his physical conditioning, his work in the batting cages or in the bullpen, batting practice, his mental preparation, and personal game planning. These things are under the control of the player's thoughts, emotions, and actions, so this is why they are part of the process of playing the game.

2. *During the Game*—This is the time when the player follows through on his preparation and seeks to execute, to get the job done, between the lines. The player's process during the game is intended to maintain positive self-confidence and effective emotional intensity, as well as to help keep his mind in the moment from pitch to pitch. This consistency of process focus during the game leads to consistent performance. Paying attention to the process as the game unfolds is under the control of the player's thoughts, emotions, and actions.

3. *After the Game*—This is the time when the player takes responsibility for how he evaluates his performance and how he uses performance feedback information to get better. Again, accurate self-evaluation is an area that has to do with the process and is under the control of the player.

Whenever a player is consistent with his performance, you usually will find a player who is prepared to compete, who is competitive on the field, and who learns from his performance. The player is consistent with his focus on the process of playing the game and not on his outcomes.

This player usually will have a well-defined process that encompasses what he has to do before the game, during the contest, and after it. He has taken charge of the process and does not leave things to chance.

More basically, this player's focus is on the process and not outcomes. He is not thinking, but proceeding to play (processing) through the game with his mind in the moment and on the task at hand.

Consistent hitters typically have a well-defined process; consistent pitchers do likewise.

When a player's focus is on the process and not on the outcomes of the process, then expected results are likely to happen for the player, more often than not.

Alternatively, when the player's focus is primarily on outcomes, and even if a good process may be in place, inconsistency of results is likely to happen to his performance, more often than not. This is so because the player's mind is not in the moment. Rather, his attention is typically on results.

As I will discuss in detail in some of the following chapters, when the player's mind is on outcomes, then tension increases and performance typically becomes inconsistent.

MORE EXAMPLES OF THE PROCESS

In life, there are many individuals who are in performance type of work, besides baseball, and who rely on a process in order to produce results or bring about accomplishments.

Examples where reliance on a systematic process leads to performance accomplishments include ones like a commercial airline pilot when flying an airplane to its destination safely and on time. The pilot files a flight plan, monitors the plane during flight, makes necessary adjustments in flight, and evaluates whether the flight went as expected when landed.

A supervisor in a manufacturing plant relies on a process when helping with the manufacturing of an automobile, according to specifications. An insurance broker uses a process in selling insurance to the right clients in an appropriate amount.

In addition, a chef in a hotel uses a process to prepare and deliver meals to guests. An effective teacher uses a sound process that includes preparing their lessons, making adjustments while teaching, and then evaluating the effectiveness of their instruction.

Playing baseball, in and of itself, can be viewed as a process since the game includes steps, rules, and procedures.

The process of playing baseball involves both on and off the field dimensions all of which are aimed at accomplishments.

The *on the field* accomplishments of playing baseball are many and include ones like having good at bats, fielding your position, throwing strikes, getting on base, and other things. For each of these accomplishments, though, a process can be implemented by the player which can contribute to the results.

In addition, *off the field* accomplishments include completing pre game routines and activities, staying out of trouble in the community, and doing well in school, among other things. Each of these accomplishments also relies on a process.

THE ESSENCE OF THE PROCESS

The process of playing baseball is basic to doing your best, on and off the field.

Clearly, the process of playing baseball involves physical and fundamental sides of the game. However, being able to focus on the process of playing the game and being willing to commit to the process is very much mental and emotional in nature and scope.

In this regard, the process involves what you commit to, what you pay attention to, how you make adjustments, and how you proceed in making sure that you are the best that you can be, on and off the field.

The process involves using your thoughts, emotions, and actions to your benefit and that of your team.

The process does not address outcomes or your numbers, but is related to them.

WHERE DO OUTCOMES FIT IN?

Are outcomes important to baseball and to your game and your team's win- loss record? Should a player not be concerned with outcomes or, in other words, his numbers?

Certainly, outcomes are important in baseball and they are an integral part of the game. Individual results do contribute to the team and to winning. Consequently, outcomes are not to be short changed.

In this respect, it is not whether baseball outcomes or statistics are important or unimportant; they certainly are relevant. Rather, what is important to playing successful baseball is the process which is used by the player in order to get outcomes.

Outcomes follow from process and process leads to outcomes. You cannot have one without the other, although the process is directly under the influence of the player.

A focus on outcomes to the neglect of the process, however, places things which are under your more immediate influence—your thoughts, emotions, actions—on the back burner, possibly limiting performance.

You are more apt at affecting the process of your game, including your mental game, than you are at controlling outcomes.

THE PROCESS MINDSET

Playing the game of baseball with a focus on and commitment to the process is basic to success, on and off the field. However, this is not an easy assignment for the player. An effective process requires understanding, time, energy, and habit on the part of the player.

If you develop a process mind set to playing the game, then your performance as a baseball player is likely to get better and to become more consistent, more often than not, over the course of time.

Developing and implementing an effective process, though, involves the four levels of psychological development that we already have discussed in Chapter 2: understanding of yourself as a person; coping effectively with the things that may derail you from implementing an effective process; how you are expected to contribute to the team; and how you perform.

The remaining chapters of this book, the Complete Mental Game, are devoted to the process of playing the game, on and off the field, and how you can take charge of the process.

THE PROCESS OF PLAYING THE GAME AND ITS TIME FRAMES

If the process is important to playing baseball, then how should you go about making sure that you are developing a process mind set and shaping a focus on the process?

The before, during, and after framework which already has been shown as Figure 3.1 can be a big help to getting you into a proper process mind set as well as a process focus.

As seen in Figure 3.1, there are three periods of time in baseball when it is to your benefit to focus on the process and to separate out. These three periods of time are the following:

1. Before the game

2. During the game

3. After the game

BEFORE THE GAME

The time frame before the game, actually well before the player arrives at the ball park, is part of the process. The before the game time frame includes the period from when the player awakens, to the time when he is involved in things other than the game, until the time he gets ready to come to the ball park.

This before the game time frame also includes the periods when you arrive at the ball park and get ready to compete.

It involves how you use your time in preparing to compete including things like making sure tickets will be available for family, taking batting practice, throwing bull pen sessions, working on your fielding, spending time in the weight room, receiving treatment from the athletic trainer, review of video of the opposition, and your own mental preparation.

With the range of activities going on before the game and the many choices that can be made, a well thought out before the game process will be a valuable investment on your part. It will help you organize yourself and to stay organized as you prepare yourself to compete.

The before the game process should fit your needs and not be complicated. In the chapter of this book on mental discipline, I will discuss in detail how to decide about your pre game process.

DURING THE GAME

The time when you are competing "between the lines", naturally, is the core of the game. In and of itself, a focus on the process is basic to competitive success.

In this respect, the during the game time frame involves a number of tasks that can benefit from a process focus. These include: preparing for and having quality at bats, being actively engaged in the game while in the field, committing to one pitch at a time, separating out offense from defense, and other things.

Making sure that you have focus on the process of competing, rather than on outcomes, requires decisions about what is important for you to do and to pay attention to, between the lines.

I will discuss these things in the chapters of the book that deal with competitive follow through.

AFTER THE GAME

Now we come to the time period that may very well be the most neglected. This is the time period following the game.

In terms of process of playing the game, there are activities that need to be thought out and addressed as part of your after the game process. These include: how to disengage from competition, when to review your performance and with whom, and other matters.

I will discuss these matters in detail especially under the section which deals with accurate self-evaluation.

EXERCISES

1. Map out the activities that are important for you to do before the game. Take into account the time periods throughout the entire day. What are activities that you need to engage in so that you can make sure that you have an effective pre game process?

2. Think through the roles that you have during the game. What do you need to make sure happens for you during this time period when you are actually competing?

3. How have you dealt with the time period following the game? To what extent has this time period been organized or not?

4. Overall, how have your process focus and mentality been? When are you most susceptible to having a focus on outcomes to the neglect of the process?

CHAPTER FOUR

THE COMPLETE MENTAL GAME BLUEPRINT

The purpose of this chapter is to provide you with a blueprint of the Complete Mental Game of baseball. The blueprint then will be fleshed out in detail in the remaining chapters of the book in terms of guidelines, methods, and procedures.

The Complete Mental Game of baseball consists of the following components:

- Three (3) core mental principles

- Twelve (12) mental domains

- Self-assessment questions for each mental domain

What does a blueprint have to do with the mental side of baseball? Consider the following:

If you were building a house, you would be investing your time and money in its construction. Naturally, you would want your time and money to be well spent and you would want your house to be built to last.

You would not want to have leaks and cracks in the house or its foundation. You would want to make sure that important areas of the house are being attended to by the builder, especially as it is being constructed, and once it is built. The areas that you would want include a proper foundation for the house, approved plumbing, safe electricity and other things that make up a house. You would want the builder to take charge of the process of building the house.

During the process of building your house, I doubt that you would want to leave the task of its construction to chance. Rather, in coordination with the builder, you would use a blueprint. Based on the blueprint, you then would proceed to design the house and to oversee the building of it, step by step, according to the blueprint.

In essence, a blueprint is a plan for construction. For a house to be built so that it has value and so that it lasts, a blueprint makes clear what is going to be constructed. The blueprint identifies the important areas, or domains, that need to be addressed when building the house.

Otherwise, without a blueprint, the kind of house you want to build may not come about; or the house could be built inefficiently and quite likely at a cost which is more than you expected.

YOUR OWN MENTAL BLUEPRINT

The Complete Mental Game has a blueprint. It includes three (3) core mental principles, twelve (12) mental domains, specific mental criteria for each domain, and self-assessment questions.

The blueprint for the Complete Mental Game relies on making effective use of your thoughts, emotions, and actions which, in turn, allow you to develop and improve yourself as a baseball player.

In relying on the blueprint for the Complete Mental game as presented in this chapter, you become the builder of your mental approach to playing baseball. To guide you along the way, you can use the blueprint as a starting point for creating your own mental plan for your development of the mental side of your game. In this regard, you become your own sport psychologist and personal counselor.

The blueprint for the Complete Mental Game, when used in collaboration with the guidelines, methods, and procedures in the remaining chapters of the book, will allow you to do the following:

1. Assess your mental strengths and limitations as a baseball player in 12 mental domains. These domains reflect twelve areas that have proven important to the success of players, on and off the baseball diamond.

2. Pinpoint important areas of your mental game that you need to work on so that you will be a better player and person.

3. Use the mental domains which are discussed in the chapters

that follow to allow you to develop and improve your mental game, by working on specific areas in more detail.

THE THREE CORE MENTAL PRINCIPLES

Let's start looking over the blueprint by considering the three core mental principles of the Complete Mental Game. These are:

1. Quality Preparation *(Before the Game)*

2. Competitive Follow Through *(During the Game)*

3. Accurate Self-Evaluation *(After the Game)*

The baseball player must make a strong commitment to these principles and to being actively involved in three very important time periods.

As we have already discussed in Chapter 3, when you pay attention to these three time periods—before, during, and after—you are focusing your thoughts, emotions, and actions on the process of playing the game. In essence, you are taking charge of the process.

In this current chapter, Chapter 4, these three time periods are presented as basic parts of the blueprint for the Complete Mental Game

The commitment that you make to these three time periods—before, during, and after—will help you to center your thoughts, emotions, and actions on things that matter to your performance and on factors that you can control and influence.

For each time period there is a core mental principle. The three core mental principles for the Complete Mental Game are the following:

Core Mental Principle I: **Quality Preparation** *(the "Before the Game" time period)*—This principle has to do with being ready to compete, and it is especially relevant before the game begins. Based on this principle, your preparation for playing baseball merits a systematic approach and focused attention, both on and off the field. Your preparation cannot be left to chance. If you want to be the best baseball performer possible, then you have to prepare to compete in a quality way.

Core Mental Principle II: **Competitive Follow Through** *(the "During the Game" time period)*—This principle states that competing effectively throughout the game will be enhanced by keeping your mind in the moment and on the immediate task at hand, one pitch at a time, and by not focusing on outcomes. Based on this principle, the more consistent that you can remain focused and composed on the process of playing the game, the greater is the likelihood that you will be competitive. In this sense, you are competitive when you have an effect on the opposition, when the opponent needs to take you into account.

Core Mental Principle III: **Accurate Self-Evaluation** *(the "After the Game" time period)*—This principle emphasizes that the task of maintaining and improving your performance requires you to be an accurate self-evaluator. Being an accurate self-evaluator reflects a willingness on your part to consider both the pluses and the minuses of your performance, and then to make necessary adjustments based on that evaluation. Being honest about your performance, what you did well and not so well, will help you to maintain consistent performance and to improve inconsistent performance.

Figure 4.1 shows the three core mental principles of the Complete Mental Game.

Figure 4.1: The three core mental principles.

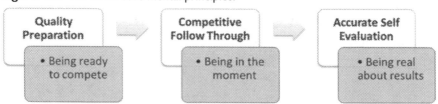

Below, each core mental principle is discussed further.

CORE MENTAL PRINCIPLE I: QUALITY PREPARATION
The core mental principle of Quality Preparation has to do with how you get yourself ready to compete before the game begins.

Before the game begins, quality preparation involves being clear with yourself about what you are going to do—mentally, physically, and fundamentally—in order to get yourself ready for game competition.

Quality preparation reflects how you accomplish the things that will get you ready to compete, and then knowing why you are engaging in these activities. Some of these pregame activities will occur in the clubhouse area; some will occur on the field; and some activities may even take place at home.

The principle of quality preparation rests on the belief that a player, who prepares for the game with a purpose, and with a step by step process before the game, will be more effective in his performance than a player with poor preparation.

CORE MENTAL PRINCIPLE II: COMPETITIVE FOLLOW THROUGH

The core mental principle of Competitive Follow Through has to do with the actual time period during which the game is being played.

Competitive follow through has to do with how you proceed to engage yourself in the game from the first pitch, and then as the game moves forward, inning by inning, to its completion. The task here involves how you can sustain an effective level of competitiveness.

In this regard, competitiveness is the extent to which you are able to have an effect on the opposition and thereby contribute to your team: Is the opposition concerned with your presence at bat, on the mound, or in the field? Do the opposing players feel you and your energy? Is the coach of the other team concerned about your presence in the lineup? If you can answer yes to these questions, you are likely to be a competitor.

Competitive follow through reflects how you engage yourself in the process of the game and how you apply your thoughts, emotions, and actions to the game; how you focus on the moment of the game and on each pitch; and how you go about making adjustments.

The principle of competitive follow through presumes that you will compete more effectively, and sustain your competitiveness more consistently, when your mind is calm and in the moment, pitch to pitch.

CORE MENTAL PRINCIPLE III: ACCURATE SELF-EVALUATION

The core mental principle of Accurate Self-Evaluation has to do with the time period after the game is completed.

Accurate self-evaluation involves how you make judgments about your game performance and how you use that information to make adjustments in your game.

Accurate self-evaluation requires that you use the evaluation of your performance and your results to learn about yourself and to get better as a player. An accurate self-evaluator deals with the facts, and does not deny his shortcomings.

The principle of accurate self-evaluation rests on a conviction that you will be better off by being honest and accurate about your performance than not.

THE TWELVE MENTAL DOMAINS

For each one of the three core mental principles—Quality Preparation, Competitive Follow Through, and Accurate Self-Evaluation—there are corresponding mental domains—twelve mental domains in all.

For each mental domain, there are specific mental criteria and self-assessment questions. You can use these criteria and questions to help you decide what are the domains of your mental game that you need to work on or that you need to learn more about.

An overview of the twelve mental domains is presented below. Then, each mental domain will be covered, in depth, as one of the remaining chapters of the book.

CORE MENTAL PRINCIPLE I: QUALITY PREPARATION

There are four mental domains that are closely associated with the core mental principle of Quality Preparation. These four mental domains are:

1. Perspective

2. Personal Awareness

3. Self-Motivation

4. Mental Discipline

Each will be discussed below.

PERSPECTIVE—BALANCING BASEBALL WITH THE REST OF MY LIFE

This domain has to do with being able to effectively balance baseball with your core personal values and with other important aspects of your life.

More specifically, perspective involves coordination of baseball with valuable aspects of your life such as your personality, family, friends, school, and spiritual beliefs, among other values.

In addition, perspective involves knowing when to "mentally park" some parts of your life, so that you can devote attention to preparing for the game and then playing it. Mental parking will allow you to enter the locker room, focused on the process of playing the game, so that you can get ready to compete.

Perspective also involves being able to turn off being a baseball player when the game is over so that you can more fully live your life.

There are five mental criteria which have to do with your perspective on baseball and life.

For each of these mental criteria, you also will find self-assessment questions. These self-assessment questions are written directly to you. As you read each of these mental criteria and the self-assessment questions that go along with them, check yourself out on each one and think about what work you need to do to get better in that particular area.

1. I am able to clarify the values which are at the core of my life. Examples of core personal values are: being responsible to my family; being a compassionate person; obtaining a good education; respecting others; having a strong commitment to my spiritual beliefs or religion; and being a good competitor and teammate. *Self-Assessment: Have I clarified my values recently? Do I know what my core personal values are?*

2. I understand how playing baseball needs to be coordinated with my core personal values so that conflicts between these two areas are eliminated. *Self-Assessment: To what extent does playing baseball conflict with other parts of my life? Have I hurt or disappointed anyone, especially family or friends, by not addressing their interests and needs?*

3. I am able to identify the people, places, and things in my life who will help and support me and who will not hinder my personal or baseball development. Examples of these

people may be mother, father, brothers and sisters, friends, advisors, and former coaches or teachers. *Self-Assessment: Who are the people in my life whom I can trust? What are the places that are good for me to frequent? What things do I want to be part of?*

4. I can pinpoint the people, places, and things that may derail me from my values and from playing baseball, and I am able to stay away from them. Examples are: drug dealers, "hangers-on", bars and clubs, alcohol, drugs, and performance enhancing supplements. *Self-Assessment: Who are the people who are not out for my best interests? What places should I avoid? What things, including drugs and other substances, are best for me to avoid altogether?*

5. I have a clear idea of what I want to accomplish as a person and as a baseball player. I am able to state what I want to accomplish in baseball and life, and I understand why I feel this way. *Self-Assessment: What do I want to be recognized for as a person? When I am finished playing baseball, what do I want to be known for?*

Guidelines, methods and procedures for developing and improving yourself in the mental domain of Perspective are found in Chapter 5.

PERSONAL AWARENESS—KNOWING MY STRONG POINTS AND LIMITATIONS AS A BASEBALL PLAYER AND A PERSON

Personal awareness has to do with understanding your strong points, adequacies, and limitations at four levels of psychological development.

These four levels are: (a) as a Person, (b) as a "Coper", that is, as someone who can deal effectively with risk, (c) as a Teammate, and (d) as a Performer.

Personal awareness includes getting a good understanding of yourself at each one of these levels. It means learning about the extent to which your thoughts, emotions, and actions help or limit you at each level.

Personal awareness means knowing what to work on that will make you a better player and person, over the short term of the game as well as over the longer haul of the season and your baseball career.

The mental criteria that are part of the personal awareness domain are the following:

1. I am willing to be honest with myself as a person, off the field, as well as a performer, on the baseball diamond. *Self-Assessment: Have I been willing to recognize my shortcomings as a person? Am I a good judge of how I perform on the baseball diamond?*

2. I am able to conduct an honest and accurate assessment of my personal strong points and limitations. *Self-Assessment: Have I recently conducted an assessment of myself as a person? Have I been honest doing this? Are there aspects of myself that I need to address?*

3. I am able to conduct an assessment of my strong points and limitations in the physical, mental, and fundamental areas of playing the game. *Self-Assessment: Have I taken the time to assess myself as a baseball player in an accurate way? Have I taken responsibility for what I have found out?*

4. I am willing to share the current assessment of myself as a baseball player with my coaches and others whom I trust. *Self-Assessment: Have I taken the time to review what I think about my game with others? Am I able to listen to and receive the feedback about my game that I get from my coaches?*

5. I am able to specify the limitations that I need to work on so that I can overcome them and become better, both on the field and off it. *Self-Assessment: Do I know what I need to work on in order to become a better player? Do I have a plan for my baseball development?*

The mental domain of Personal Awareness is covered in detail in Chapter 6 of the book.

SELF-MOTIVATION—PURSUING GOALS THAT ARE IMPORTANT TO MY SUCCESS IN BASEBALL AND BEYOND

Self-motivation is reflected in how passionate you are about playing baseball and about life in general.

Self-motivation involves settings goals that are important for your success, both on and off the baseball diamond, and then pursuing those goals enthusiastically and with purposeful effort.

Self-motivation translates into doing things each and every day, before, during and after the game, so that you are more consistent in your performance and more successful in your life.

The mental criteria which are part of the self-motivation domain are the following:

1. I am able to identify goals that, if I make progress toward them, will make me a better overall baseball player and person. **Self-Assessment**: *Have I spent time in setting goals for my success in baseball? To what extent are these goals ones which I can influence and control through my effort?*

2. I make sure that the goals which I set for myself are SMART: S-Specific; M-Measurable; A-Attainable, R-Relevant; and T-Time framed. **Self-Assessment**: *Are my goals ones that are important to my development and success as a baseball player? Are my goals ones which I can influence and control and which will make me a better performer? Are my goals SMART?*

3. I can follow through with the drills and activities that will allow me to attain my goals. **Self-Assessment**: *Have I identified the actions that I need to take in order to make progress toward my goals? Do I have a way of evaluating the attainment of my goals and my effort?*

4. I can challenge myself about why I am playing the game and how I am competing. **Self-Assessment**: *Have I taken the time to really examine why I play baseball? Do my reasons for playing baseball motivate me?*

5. I am willing to find out how other players, especially veteran players, keep themselves motivated to play the game. **Self-**

Assessment: *Do I have any players who are role models for me? Have I learned about playing the game from watching and talking to other players?*

The guidelines, methods, and procedures that will help you develop and improve in the mental domain of Self-Motivation are described in Chapter 7 of the book.

MENTAL DISCIPLINE—HAVING A PLAN AND FOLLOWING THROUGH WITH IT

Mental discipline is the fourth mental domain of the Complete Mental Game. Mental discipline involves how you go about planning what you want to accomplish for each game and also how you realize those accomplishments, before and during the game.

Mental discipline also involves your longer range preparation, including career planning, continuing education, and other areas which are relevant to you.

The mental criteria for the mental discipline domain are the following:

1. I have a long range plan for my development as a baseball player. This is a plan that includes the physical, mental, and fundamental areas. *Self-Assessment*: *Do I have a long range plan for my development as a baseball player? Am I committed to this kind of plan?*

2. I have a pre-game routine that is effective for me and I follow through with it. *Self-Assessment*: *Do I have an effective pregame routine? How consistent am I in following through with my pregame routine?*

3. I monitor the follow through of my plans and routines. *Self-Assessment*: *Do I monitor myself on my mental discipline? Do I have a way of identifying when I start to slack off on my plans and routines?*

4. I challenge myself when I recognize that I am not disciplined enough and then I make necessary adjustments. *Self-Assessment*: *Am I willing to let myself know that I am not following through with my plans? Do I start off with good intentions about my plan but I do not follow through?*

5. I adjust my plans and routines, based on facts and results. *Self-Assessment: Have I made adjustments to my plans and routines based on whether they are working for me? Have I been honest with myself about my mental discipline?*

The domain of Mental Discipline is presented in Chapter 8 of the book with respect to guidelines, methods, and procedures.

CORE MENTAL PRINCIPLE II: COMPETITIVE FOLLOW THROUGH

There are five mental domains that are aligned with the core mental principle of Competitive Follow Through. These five mental domains are the following:

1. Self-Confidence

2. Emotional Intensity

3. Focus

4. Composure

5. Teamwork

SELF CONFIDENCE—BELIEVING IN MY SKILLS AND ABILITIES TO EXECUTE AND TO GET THE JOB DONE ON THE BASEBALL DIAMOND

Self-confidence has to do with your beliefs. It reflects how you think about your performance, along with the extent to which you feel that you are going to execute, between the lines. This is the case no matter what your position or role on your team.

Self-confidence also is reflected in how you view your baseball career over the long haul: Do you believe that you will make the team? That you will be successful? That you will advance to the next level of play?

The mental criteria that are part of the domain of self-confidence are the following:

1. I know what I want to accomplish for each game. I can visualize what I am going to accomplish. *Self-Assessment: Do I know what I want to accomplish? Can I see and feel this and do I feel good about doing so?*

2. I monitor my confidence level before the game, and as the game proceeds, and I make adjustments to my confidence as necessary. *Self-Assessment*: *Am I able to recognize when my confidence starts to waver? Can I adjust to get my confidence back?*

3. I play the game with positive body language, no matter how I feel at any point in time during the game. *Self-Assessment*: *Do I know what I look like when I am confident in my role on the baseball diamond? Do I recognize what it feels like when I am confident?*

4. I can determine the times during the game when my self-confidence is most vulnerable and take steps to not let those situations lessen my confidence. *Self-Assessment*: *Am I aware of when I am most likely to lose my confidence and how this happens? Do I have a way to get my confidence back to an effective level?*

5. I know what I need to say and to think so that my confidence remains positive. *Self-Assessment*: *Am I aware of what I say to myself or think about that allows me to be confident?*

Chapter 9 of the book covers methods and procedures that you can apply to boost and maintain yourself in the mental domain of Self Confidence.

EMOTIONAL INTENSITY—GIVING CONSISTENT ENERGY AND EFFORT THROUGHOUT THE GAME

Emotional intensity represents the energy and effort which you give, as you compete, during the game. This mental domain reflects how you feel when you compete and how you go about competing, pitch to pitch.

Emotional intensity is important to your performance throughout the contest, as the game begins and then up and until the last pitch. It involves being able to play the game with an amount of emotion that is effective for you, the player—not too much, yet not too little.

The mental criteria which are associated with emotional intensity are the following:

1. I am able to make myself aware of the level of emotion that

will get me ready to compete and the amount of emotion that can keep me from being competitive. *Self-Assessment*: *Do I have a way to recognize when my energy and effort are lower than necessary? Do I know what it feels like when my intensity level is right for me?*

2. I can detect when my emotions are too high or too low and then get them back to an even level. *Self-Assessment*: *How do I use my emotions? When does lack of intensity do me in and affect my performance for the worst?*

3. I am able to recognize when I am not giving my best effort and I can quickly get myself back on course. *Self-Assessment*: *Do I tend to deny when I am not giving my best effort? When I am not really trying, how do I adjust?*

4. I want to feel energetic and competitive when I am in the lineup, with good emotional intensity. *Self-Assessment*: *Am I ready to play the game at an effective level of emotional intensity? How do I get into and remain in this state?*

The guidelines, methods, and procedures for developing in the mental domain of Emotional Intensity are included in Chapter 10 of the book.

FOCUS—KEEPING MY MIND IN THE MOMENT AND ON THE TASK AT HAND
Focus is at the center of your mental approach to playing baseball. Focus has to do with being competitive, pitch to pitch. In this respect, focus involves paying attention to what is important in the moment with respect to the upcoming pitch and for only that task.

Focus involves being able to let go of everything and dealing solely with the task at hand, which is the next pitch. This is the case whether you are a pitcher, fielder, hitter, or base runner.

The mental criteria which are associated with the domain of focus are the following:

1. I am able to concentrate my attention, pitch by pitch, on the task at hand. *Self-Assessment*: *When I am focused, do I know what gets me this way? When are the times when my focus is the best?*

2. I recognize the thoughts and emotions which can distract me and which result in loss of my concentration, and then I can quickly get my mind back into the moment. *Self-Assessment*: *What are the things that I say and do which cause me to lose my focus? What are the game situations when I tend to allow my focus to waver?*

3. I am able to shift my attention from a broad focus like getting signs from the third base coach to a narrow focus where I focus in on the next pitch. *Self-Assessment*: *How good am I in shifting my focus from broad to narrow and back? Do I recognize the times and situations when I do not need to focus?*

4. I have a pre pitch routine which allows me the opportunity to take a de-focus break, between pitches. *Self-Assessment*: *How do I handle myself between pitches? Do I have a routine that I can use between pitches to de-focus?*

5. I embrace the challenge of being engrossed in the game, one pitch at a time. *Self-Assessment*: *Do I enjoy keeping myself engaged in the game? When do I enjoy playing the game the most?*

The mental domain of Focus is covered in detail in Chapter 11 of the book.

COMPOSURE—REMAINING POISED UNDER COMPETITIVE PRESSURE

This domain deals with your being able to effectively cope with challenging game situations and remaining poised during them. These are situations when the game is on the line as well as game situations when you could easily let your emotions get away from you.

The domain of composure involves being able to recognize ineffective emotions and to regroup, in the moment. The mental criteria for composure are the following:

1. I can identify the game situations when I tend to become tense, anxious, and stressed. *Self-Assessment*: *When are the times and game situations when I tend to lose my composure? What do I do and say to myself during those times?*

2. I am able to keep my mind in the moment when things on the field are not going right for me. *Self-Assessment*: *How effective am I in staying in the moment and dealing with the upcoming pitch? What takes my mind out of the moment?*

3. I can accept game situations and feelings which I am experiencing and not get caught up in them. *Self-Assessment*: *How well do I observe myself as I perform rather than judging myself? Do I get caught up in thinking about outcomes rather than the process?*

4. I can implement a routine which allows me to de-compress and regroup, when I start to feel pressure. *Self-Assessment*: *When I start to feel pressed, how do I let that feeling go? What do I say to myself and what actions do I take that keep me composed?*

5. I am able to get my thinking back into the moment when I start to lose my composure. *Self-Assessment*: *What does it feel like when I am composed? When I lose my composure?*

The mental domain of Composure is covered in Chapter 12 of the book.

TEAMWORK—INTERACTING PRODUCTIVELY WITH TEAMMATES, COACHES, AND OTHERS

The mental domain of Teamwork has to do with being able to relate productively to others while the game is going on. In this sense, you work as part of the team.

Teamwork requires communication and a willingness to adapt with teammates, coaches, athletic trainers, umpires, fans, and others.

Under certain conditions, teamwork involves being a leader. The mental criteria for teamwork are the following:

1. I can cooperate with my teammates so that we can get the job done on the field (e.g., working together on cut off and relays; turning the double play). *Self-Assessment*: *What kind of teammate have I been? What would other players think of me as a teammate?*

2. I am able to communicate clearly and specifically with my teammates so that each one of us knows what the other is doing. *Self-Assessment*: *As a teammate do I communicate effectively with teammates? When I have a problem with a coach or a teammate, how have I handled these situations?*

3. I relate appropriately and respectfully with umpires about their calls. *Self-Assessment*: *What do umpires think of me? What has been my approach to relating to umpires?*

4. I deal respectfully and constructively with coaches and other persons when things do not go my way. *Self-Assessment*: *What have coaches and instructors thought of me? What is my approach for relating to coaches?*

5. I am willing to assume a leadership role with teammates, as necessary and appropriate, given my role on the team. *Self-Assessment*: *To what extent have I been a leader on my team? How have I taken the lead in influencing with my teammates?*

You can review Chapter 13 of the book for guidelines and procedures that have to do with the mental domain of Teamwork.

CORE MENTAL PRINCIPLE III: ACCURATE SELF-EVALUATION

There are three mental domains that are grouped under the third core mental principle of Accurate Self-Evaluation. These three domains are the following:

1. Self-Esteem

2. Performance Accountability

3. Continuous Improvement

SELF-ESTEEM—SEPARATING MY PERFORMANCE AS A PLAYER FROM MYSELF AS A PERSON

Your self-esteem is a real personal matter. In this respect, self-esteem has to do with being a good separator. It involves how you size yourself up as a person and as a performer and how you keep those areas separate.

Self-esteem has to do with your willingness to be truthful and humble about what you do and why. It involves being able to stay on an even keel about yourself, no matter how you perform.

When your self-esteem is good, you do not get a big head when you do well and you do not over inflate your ego. In contrast, if you do not perform well, you do not beat yourself up. You can keep things separate.

The mental criteria for the domain of self-esteem are the following:

1. I can keep my game performance in perspective and do not get personal with it. *Self-Assessment: When have I let my performance affect my personal life? What did I say to myself and do to allow this to happen?*

2. I do not inflate myself (get a big head) when my performances are productive. *Self-Assessment: How do I react when I am performing well? What do I have to watch out for about myself when things are going well on the field?*

3. I do not deflate myself (beat myself up mentally) when my performance does not proceed as expected. *Self-Assessment: How do I react when I am not performing well? What do I have to be aware of when things are not going well for me on the field?*

4. I recognize that, during the course of the season, I will have good days and not so good days on the baseball diamond. *Self-Assessment: How do I deal with the day to day demands of the baseball season? When I am most vulnerable to being hard on myself during the season?*

5. I am able to pay attention to the process of playing the game and get satisfaction from it, no matter what my results. *Self-Assessment: When are the times when I focus my attention*

on outcomes and forget about the process? What does the process of playing the game of baseball mean to me?

Guidelines, methods, and procedures for the mental domain of Self- Esteem are discussed in Chapter 14 of the book.

PERFORMANCE ACCOUNTABILITY—TAKING RESPONSIBILITY FOR MY PERFORMANCE

Performance accountability has to do with being ready, willing, and able to take responsibility for your results.

It involves being accountable for how you perform. Performance accountability does not include looking for excuses when things do not go well in your performance on the field as well as in other aspects of your life.

Performance accountability requires skills in pinpointing the pluses and minuses of your game performance and for what you pay attention to. It also involves knowing the reasons that your performance has gone as expected or not as expected.

The mental criteria for the domain of Performance Accountability are the following:

1. I take the time following each game to review how I performed and I do this in a systematic way. *Self-Assessment: How committed have I been in reviewing my performance? When do I find is the best time and the worst time to think about how I am performing on the baseball diamond?*

2. I can pinpoint the pluses and minuses of my performance in an accurate way and I understand why things are this way. *Self-Assessment: When I evaluate my performance, I am humble and honest about my strong points—physically, mentally, fundamentally? When I look at my limitations, how honest and specific have I been?*

3. I am willing to obtain and use feedback from coaches and instructors about my performance. *Self-Assessment: What are the times and situations when I tend to become defensive about my performance? When I receive feedback from my coaches, how focused am I on listening to what is being said to me?*

4. I can keep my emotions in check when reviewing, seeking, and using feedback about my performance. *Self-Assessment*: *When and under what conditions do I get emotional when someone is talking about my game? How do I use the information that coaches provide me about my performance?*

The guidelines, methods, and procedures for the mental domain of Performance Accountability are included in Chapter 15 of the book.

Continuous Improvement—striving to get better, both on the baseball diamond and off of it

Continuous improvement has to do with how you use the information at your disposal about your performance, your baseball career, and your life.

Every baseball player is encouraged to consider baseball as a never ending process that demands adjustments and improvements.

Nothing in the game or in life stays the same. You are either moving ahead or changing, or you are stagnating.

It involves making decisions about what to do next, what adjustments to make, what you have learned and how you can get better.

Continuous improvement includes the short term and longer haul. It encompasses the next game, the next series, and other things.

The mental criteria which are associated with continuous improvement are the following:

1. I am willing to take stock of myself about where I stand in my game and in life, with honestly and accuracy. *Self-Assessment*: *Have I thought about my baseball career and what follows it?*

2. I can use information about myself as a person and as a performer to adjust and improve myself, on and off the baseball diamond. **Self-Assessment**: *How do I learn best? How do I use information about myself in order to get better?*

3. I have a plan for the next steps in my baseball career. *Self-Assessment*: *What is my plan for my career, on and off the baseball diamond? Have I spent time on this area?*

4. I recognize when it is time to transition out of the game as a player. *Self-Assessment: If my baseball career were to end soon, what will I do next in my life?*

The mental domain of Continuous Improvement is covered in Chapter 16 of the book.

EXERCISES

1. How have you gone about preparing for games? What have you been good at in terms of your preparation? What are things that you need to improve upon?

2. How do you compete from pitch to pitch? What are you good at here? What are your limitations?

3. To what extent are you an accurate evaluator of your performance? What will make you better as a self-evaluator?

PART TWO

QUALITY PREPARATION: BEING READY TO COMPETE

CHAPTER FIVE

— ⚾ —

PERSPECTIVE: BALANCING BASEBALL WITH YOUR LIFE

Perspective is the first of the twelve mental domains of the Complete Mental Game. Perspective is the first domain covered because it is basic to success in baseball and in life.

Without perspective, you are at a distinct disadvantage, on and off the baseball diamond. With perspective, you are better able to put things that happen to you on and off the field, in their proper place, mentally and emotionally, and to deal with them accordingly.

Perspective has to do with being able to place baseball into the fiber and fabric of your life. It involves taking the game of baseball, clarifying your values, and balancing it effectively with other important parts of your life.

These other important parts of your life may include things like being actively involved with your family, continuing your education, adhering to religious or spiritual beliefs, involving yourself in community projects, following through on business interests, or other things.

Perspective involves putting baseball into a proper place for you and for the important people in your life, such as your family, based on your personal values. When you have things in perspective, you are better prepared, mentally and emotionally, to compete and to get the job done, between the lines.

WHEN TO CHECK ON YOUR PERSPECTIVE

You can conduct a self-assessment of your perspective at any time during the year or even during the baseball season. However, there are two times frames during the year which have proven useful times for reviewing perspective.

One particular time frame for conducting a self-assessment of your perspective is during the off season or the winter months when you are not actively playing baseball. This is a good period of time to reflect on where you are in your career and where you are going with it, since you are not actively involved in games.

In addition, another good time to check yourself out on your perspective is during the baseball season when you sense that things are getting out of balance for you. This may be a period of time when you become frustrated and confused about how your career is going and you do not know why you feel that way. You may feel stale and sense that you are getting little out of the game, or you question your desire to play the game.

ADVANTAGES TO YOU WHEN YOU HAVE THINGS IN PERSPECTIVE

There are many distinct advantages to your overall mental and emotional development as a baseball player for being able to keep things in perspective. These advantages include the following:

1. Perspective enables you to be thankful for the natural talent that you have been given for playing baseball. Everyone is not able to play the game and everyone does not have a knack for it or interest in baseball. Perspective allows you to be appreciative of the opportunities which you have had to develop your talent and skills and to play the game of baseball. Every baseball player does not have equal amounts of talent or opportunities. So, whatever talent and skills you do possess, hold yourself responsible for using and developing them.

2. With perspective, it is easier to keep your mind centered on the reality that there is more to life than baseball. This broad vantage point enables you to recognize that, although baseball is a very important part of your life, there are other things that take precedence over baseball, such as your family or your education. Here is a statement which has to

do with perspective and which is something for you to think about: *There is more to life than baseball, but there also is more to baseball than baseball.*

3. Having a good perspective allows you to recognize what really is important to you in baseball, and to identify the things that are important that are over and above the game. This recognition will provide you with a peace of mind, which is a mindset that is calm and which allows you to focus on the process of playing the game. In this regard, a good perspective will help you get ready to play each game and to remain in a positive frame of mind throughout the season.

4. Keeping things in perspective, on and off the baseball diamond, also helps to minimize personal distractions. These can be distractions that may derail your career, like alcohol, drugs and other substances. With perspective, personal distractions are minimized and do not harm you because the things that are important to your life—your core personal values—have been identified and clarified. This kind of perspective allows you to commit to those values and to let other things go. Baseball, then, takes its proper place in your life.

5. When you have a good perspective, you are more likely to respect the game including its traditions, norms, and players, as well as the process of playing it. This respect gives you a chance to enjoy the game and appreciate it for what it is and for what it is not. Here is another statement for you to think about and that can help put things in perspective: *Baseball is what you do. It is not who you are.*

Think of baseball players who you know, or who you have seen play the game. They may be current players or ones who played long ago. These players could be at any level of competition. Consider which of these players in your opinion have had good perspectives and who seem to have been able to effectively coordinate playing baseball with the rest of their lives.

The chances are great that the players that you have identified with good perspectives have been able to reap the benefits of playing and they have enjoyed the process. In addition, these baseball players are likely to be ones who have gotten the most out of their natural talent and abilities, while being engaged in a quality life overall.

DISADVANTAGES OF NOT HAVING THINGS IN PERSPECTIVE

When baseball is not placed into proper perspective in a player's life, however, a personal imbalance can develop. What happens is that personal things get out of whack, day to day, like not paying attention to your education, or neglecting important people in your life.

Many times, these personal imbalances seep onto the baseball diamond and performance suffers. This can lead to difficulties for the individual player, both on and off the baseball diamond.

Disadvantages of not having things in perspective as a baseball player include the following:

1. With poor perspective, you can be very inconsiderate of other people, not just teammates, but other important people in life, like family members and close friends.

2. Lack of perspective promotes a false sense of security about your place in the game, which can result in poor decision making. Baseball is a game that can humble the player. There are many ups and downs and, when things are not in perspective, there can be a tendency to act quickly and with this impulsiveness come mistakes and negative consequences.

3. When perspective is lost, neglecting and even hurting the feelings of other people by not taking the time to consider their needs can come to the fore.

4. Limited perspective leads to being selfish and only thinking of one's needs.

5. When a good perspective is not present, you may very well miss out on satisfying experiences with other players, staff, family, and friends.

6. Losing the trust and respect of individuals and groups due to being self-centered and selfish can occur with poor perspective.

Think of baseball players who you know, or who you have read about, who you think do not seem to have things in perspective. These individuals probably have exhibited some of the qualities listed above.

CORE PERSONAL VALUES AND THEIR MEANING FOR YOU

Values are what give your life meaning, on and off the baseball diamond. Values are the basic things in life that are important to you and they are basic to having a good perspective.

Values are statements about you and your life. They are not tangible and cannot be seen or measured. Rather, values are intangible, ongoing, and priceless.

When a baseball player says that he has a passion for playing the game of baseball, the player has stated a value about himself. When another player indicates that he wants to make sure that he receives his college degree, this shows that he values education. When a teammate states that he wants to be kind and decent to other people, this also is a value statement about his concern for others.

Values are not actions or behaviors. However, actions and behaviors are linked to values. What gives your personal values clarity and effectiveness are your actions and behaviors—the way that you live out those values, day to day.

Stating that you have a passion for playing the game of baseball is a value statement. Playing the game hard—preparing, competing, and making adjustments—day in and day out, illustrates that your passion for playing the game is operating as part of your life. Your values and actions are linked.

When you register and complete the final courses that you need for a degree and successfully complete them, you have given some specific meaning to the value which you have placed on education.

CLARIFYING YOUR CORE PERSONAL VALUES

Values are the building blocks for developing and maintaining a proper perspective on baseball and your life. However, to play out and live out your values, you first need to know what your core personal values are. You need to clarify them. This task cannot be left to chance.

To get at your core personal values, the process of values clarification can be useful for you.

Values clarification is a process that enables you to spend time identifying the important things to you—the values which are at the core of your life.

There are some specific steps that you can take to clarify your values, first as a person and then as a baseball player.

You can use the "Values Clarification Form", which is seen as Figure 5.1, to help you to follow through on these steps.

Figure 5.1: Values Clarification Form.

	Values	Reasons	Behaviors
1.			
2.			
3.			
4.			
5.			

Here are steps which you can take in clarifying your core personal values:

1. Identify the most important things in your life, the things that are at the core of your life; the things that make life meaningful for you. The things which you identify can be considered as your core personal values. Some examples are: continuing my education; communicating with my family and spending time with them; helping people in need; paying attention to the spiritual side of life; using my talent to play baseball to the fullest; playing the game of baseball the right way; or other things that give life meaning.

2. Challenge yourself as to *why* each of the values that you have listed is important and is at the core in your life. Make sure that you spend time thinking about the reasons. Do not shortchange yourself with this step.

3. Identify the behaviors and actions which you can take that will allow you to live out these life values, day to day, on and off the baseball diamond. These are the concrete things that you do which are examples of living out your values.

Table 5.1 is an example illustration of how personal and baseball values were clarified by a major league player using the Values Clarification Form.

TABLE 5.1. Example of a completed values clarification form of a Major League player.

	Values	Reasons	Behaviors
1.	Quality Family Life	My family is at the core of my life	• Listen • Be active with them • Follow through on plans
2.	Giving to others less fortunate	Appreciation and gratitude for what I have in the game	• Set up charitable foundation
3.	Faith	Give thanks for my life and for what I have in the game.	• Read Bible • Attend services with family • Believe
4.	Baseball	This is my profession	• Play the game the right way

STAYING BALANCED

It is often said that baseball is a game of failure. If you have played the game long enough, I am pretty sure that you have heard baseball being referred to in this manner. In fact, it would be very surprising if you have not experienced failure on a number of occasions.

If you get three hits in every ten at bats, you are doing very well no matter what the level of competition. However, there are seven other at bats that may not have gone so well in which you have made out.

A pitcher may have a very good outing throwing quality pitches and getting batters out. However, this pitcher can still wind up getting a loss for the game.

In order to get to the major leagues, it can take many years. Some of those years may be good ones, while others may be filled with adversity; an injury can set back your career.

Playing baseball can easily be a negative experience—if you allow it to be. Since baseball is a game of failure, it is helpful to have a way of counteracting that kind of trend.

It is helpful to maintain an effective balance of your perspective when things are going well and when things that are not going as planned.

Staying in balance, and checking out whether you are in personal balance, is an important skill to learn as part of the perspective domain.

Here are some ways to stay in balance as a baseball player and as a person who plays baseball:

1. Write down ten things about baseball and your life that you are thankful for and which you appreciate. These things may be ones like: having a supportive family environment; a loving mother; being exposed to good coaching; having outstanding natural talent; being able to travel; being around teammates; or other things.

2. Reflect on what each of these things mean to your game and life. Why are you thankful for them? What do you appreciate about each one?

3. Now, think back over the past six to ten months or so. Within that time frame, select one or two baseball experiences that you have been proud of. These experiences may have to do with a game performance, getting help from a veteran player, or helping someone else who is learning to play the game. Spend some time reflecting on these things and why they have been important to you.

4. Whenever you start to feel down, and when you start to

feel yourself lose your personal balance, step back and do an appreciation check. This is a way for you to regain perspective and good personal balance. Think of the things that you have identified above under steps 1, 2, and 3. Center yourself on the thoughts and the feelings of appreciation which comes with them. Place baseball back into perspective with your life.

DEALING WITH RISK

Another important part of the perspective domain is knowing your personal risk factors. These are factors which can derail you from being the best that you can be, if you do not address them. These are the factors which can put you at personal risk.

Also it is important to know your supportive factors. These are factors which will support you and keep you on track as a baseball player and as a person.

As part of the Complete Mental Game, knowing your risk and supportive factors involves knowing your PPTs.

PPTs is an abbreviation for three factors which you need to have a way to deal with as a baseball player and person. These are:

P: People

P: Places

T: Things

In order to get a handle on your PPTs, you can use the "Risk and Support Factors Form". A copy of this form is seen as Figure 5.2.

Figure 5.2: Risk and Support Factors Form. List the people, places, and things that can pull you in the *wrong direction (risks)* and *positive direction (supports)*.

Risks (-)	Factors	Supports (+)
	People	
	Places	
	Things	

Here are steps which you can take in identifying your risk factors or negative PPTs:

1. Identify the types of *people* who you do not want to be associated with in baseball and life. These are the individuals who are likely to have a negative effect on you and your perspective and who enable you to get out of balance. These negative people can be ones such as drug dealers, individuals who want money from you, and other people who do not have your best interests at heart. Specify how you are going to stay away from these people.

2. Identify the *places* which you want to avoid. These may be places like bars and clubs, street corners, hallways in school, or other places which would place you in compromising positions. Here too, specify why you want to avoid them and how you are going to do this.

3. Identify the *things* which are not good for you and which you do not want to take or otherwise ingest. Examples are drugs of abuse, steroids and amphetamines and other substances. Make a commitment to say no to these things.

Now, let us get to the positive side of dealing with risk. This is the support side. Steps for determining your personal support system are the following:

1. List the *people* whom you are sure that you trust. These are the people who are in your corner and who will be there for you, no matter what.

2. Identify the *places* that are safe and secure and which are locations which will add to your baseball development and life.

3. Specify the positive *things*, over and above people and places, which you want to have as part of your life.

4. Make a concerted effort to involve your personal support system in your baseball career and your life.

MENTAL PARKING

Playing baseball is time consuming and it involves considerable energy and effort, over the course of a season. Often, one thing in a player's life can leak into another and sooner or later, the individual can be overwhelmed and out of balance.

In this regard, a baseball player needs to be a good separator. In this sense, a good separator is a player who can keep things in compartments, like the present from the past and the future.

One aspect of being a good separator, however, has to do with "mental parking". By being good with mental parking, you can contribute to your overall perspective.

Mental parking is the process of leaving your role as a person outside the clubhouse door when you have a game to get ready for and then centering your attention on the process of playing the game.

Mental parking gets this term from being able to "park" things that are not baseball related and then picking them up as you leave the game and at which time you mentally park the game.

Mental parking involves the following thoughts, emotions, and actions.

1. Committing to leaving your personal cares and concerns at the clubhouse door.

2. Being willing to put on the role of being a baseball player, while your personal cares and concerns are parked at the clubhouse door.

3. Preparing for the game and competing, with energy and enthusiasm, one pitch at a time.

4. Picking up your personal cares and concerns as you leave the clubhouse to go home.

5. Mentally parking your role as a player until you return.

EMBRACING A PERSONAL MISSION

You probably have heard the following phrase in some way when referring to successful players: "He was on a mission and no one could stop him". You may have heard this being applied to a baseball player or to some other kind of performer, including perhaps to yourself.

A mission is a way of accomplishing something that is important and which typically involves many different parts to it. Going to the moon required a mission approach. Becoming a profitable business or an effective organization requires a mission orientation.

Becoming and remaining a balanced baseball player and person involves a sense of mission. This kind of pursuit helps to firm up your perspective. The development of a personal mission, indeed embracing one, is helpful to your perspective.

DEVELOPING A PERSONAL MISSION STATEMENT

You can create a personal mission statement for yourself at any time and you can update it whenever you think it is important to do so. Here are some steps to follow:

1. Challenge yourself by asking the following questions: (a) Who are you as a player and a person? (b) What do you want to accomplish in baseball and life? (c) How do you want to be remembered as a baseball player?

2. Now, use the information from the questions on which you have challenged yourself and write a personal mission statement. Just get down the things that are important, that you want to accomplish and be remembered for.

3. Review what you have written about yourself and your mission. Make changes in it that you think will make it clearer. In reviewing what you have written consider the following: Are you happy with what you have written? Is the statement clear and specific? Does it have meaning for you? Are you motivated by what is on paper?

4. Make any necessary changes. Then, place your personal mission statement on a card or in some way that you can refer to it often. You may want to place it in your locker or

in your desk. You can look at it often and use it as a way of maintaining perspective.

Table 5.2 includes examples of personal mission statements which have been developed by some minor and major league baseball players.

TABLE 5.2. Examples of personal mission statements developed by Minor and Major League players.

- I am a left-handed pitcher who consistently gets batters out with quality pitchers.
- I am a dependable and fierce competitor. I will do all that I can to help my team, both sides of the plate.
- My success in baseball comes from being myself and from my preparation.
- I strive to be the best that I can be, pitch by pitch, day by day.
- I am a competitor. I play the game all out – with energy and no fear.

KEEPING TRACK OF YOUR PERSPECTIVE

Periodically, it is helpful to monitor your perspective. This will allow you to make sure that you are keeping baseball balanced with your life.

As you proceed with the season and even with your career, things change including your values. There can be many reasons for this and you do not want to assume anything or let it happen by chance.

Step back and make sure that your values in life are aligned with your actions so that they will support and not hinder your baseball performance.

You can make a personal appointment with yourself to review your values and your mission statement.

If you find that you are veering off course from them, you can make an adjustment and get back on track.

If you need to alter your values or personal mission, make sure you know why you need to do this and then take appropriate actions.

EXERCISES

1. What are your most important values? Write them down and list the reasons why each one is important to you and your game.

2. How do you envision yourself as a baseball player--- One year from now? Five years down the line? Ten years out from the present?

3. How do you want to be remembered as a baseball player, once your playing days are finished? Why do you want to be remembered that way?

4. Who are players in baseball that you admire and respect? Why?

5. What would you do if baseball no longer existed?

6. What do you know about the history and traditions in the game, including about former players? What can you learn here?

7. What does respecting the game mean to you?

CHAPTER SIX

––––––– ✑ –––––––

PERSONAL AWARENESS: KNOWING YOUR STRONG POINTS AND LIMITATIONS

Know Thyself! This is a phrase that was used by Socrates. He was a distinguished Greek philosopher and leader of long ago. Socrates used the phrase—know thyself—to remind government officials and business leaders that being productive in their positions started with their self- understanding.

This same saying—know thyself—made centuries ago, applies directly to you, today, as a baseball player.

If you want to become and remain a top performer in baseball, you need to know your strengths and limitations about your game and what you need to improve on. Otherwise, you are shortchanging your overall development and limiting your performance. The things that need to be addressed will not be a part of your development.

The task of knowing yourself is so important to success in playing baseball that it has been incorporated as one of the twelve mental domains of the Complete Mental Game. It is the mental domain of personal awareness.

Personal awareness is the mental domain which takes into account the extent to which you know yourself, and about yourself, on and off the baseball diamond.

Personal awareness has to do with your understanding about how you play the game and how you live your life in relation to being a baseball player and beyond. Personal awareness involves knowing about and understanding your strong points in the physical, fundamental, and mental sides of baseball as well as knowing about the things that are limiting you from getting better in these areas as a baseball player.

There is a growing body of research in cognitive development and performance psychology which indicates that individuals who are successful at their work and who perform effectively at what they do typically possess a very good understanding of themselves—their personal awareness is high.

Personal awareness means that you know your strong points and limitations as a baseball player, in all areas of your game, and as a person. These areas include your strong points and limitations for all three sides of the game including your physical conditioning, the baseball fundamentals which are relevant to your position and, of course, the mental aspects, both on and off the baseball diamond.

With a good command of your personal awareness, you will be better prepared to play the game and stay within yourself. It also will be easier for you to avoid doing things on the field that you are not capable of doing or that you have not yet become skilled at.

WHEN TO CHECK OUT YOUR PERSONAL AWARENESS

You can assess yourself in the mental domain of personal awareness at any time during the year. However, a good time for a check is before the beginning of the baseball season.

In order to prepare yourself for the upcoming season, and when necessary during the season, systematic attention to the mental domain of personal awareness is highly recommended.

REQUIREMENTS FOR PERSONAL AWARENESS

Conducting an assessment of your strengths and limitations as a baseball player, however, requires that you are honest with yourself. Honesty in this sense means that you are willing to deal with the facts about your development—where you stand and what you need to work on, no matter what they may be.

Sometimes the facts may be harsh about your development or performance and they are not what you want to hear. It comes as no surprise then that there is a tendency not to want to be honest with yourself and to look the other way. When you deny things about how you play the game that you need to improve on, you are cheating no one but yourself.

In addition, pinpointing your strong points and limitations requires that you commit to working on your game and to develop a plan for your improvement, once you conduct an assessment.

NATURE AND SCOPE OF PERSONAL AWARENESS

Personal awareness involves striving to know yourself and where you stand in terms of the development of your skills in all three sides of the game—your physical skills, fundamental skills, and mental skills.

Knowing where you stand in the skills that are part of the three sides of the game, and then being willing to deal with what you find out, can have a tremendous impact and influence on how you perform and how your baseball career takes shape.

Through personal awareness, you can better yourself in the following ways with respect to the three sides of the game:

1. You can arrive at an understanding about where you are in the development of your *physical skills*—knowing your strong points and limitations in areas such as strength, speed, endurance, flexibility, etc. This self-understanding also includes knowing what skills that you have mastered, and what is all right with your game but which can be improved.

2. You can become clear and realistic about where you stand in terms of your *fundamental skills*, given your position or role on the team. These skills may be in areas such as the fundamentals of hitting, fielding, base running, pitching, and whatever else is relevant

3. You also can get specific about where you are in terms of your *mental skills*. This includes knowing the mental areas in which you are strong, such as your focus and composure, those which are satisfactory, and what requires improvement, both on and off the baseball diamond.

This book, of course, is devoted to helping you identify your strong points and limitations in the mental side of baseball

ADVANTAGES OF BEING PERSONALLY AWARE

Spending time on developing your personal awareness is by no means a waste of time.

There are many baseball players, including a range of successful major league players, who will tell you that getting to know yourself, on and off the field, is a very valuable investment of your time.

There are a range of advantages to you in spending time in developing your personal awareness so that you can be the best that you can be.

Here are some reasons that players believe have been important to them in developing their personal awareness:

1. By being aware of your strong points and limitations, you are more ready to take advantage of your natural talent and not get sidetracked in trying to be something which is not within your skill set.

2. You can more easily commit to focusing on playing the game within yourself, while at the same time strive to improve at your game.

3. You will be in a better place to create a plan of action for your physical, fundamental, and mental skill development, since what you need to work on will be clear.

4. You are likely to have more fun playing the game, since what you currently know about yourself as a player has been specified and is not vague.

5. You can prevent yourself from overestimating or underestimating your skills and abilities. You will know where you stand with respect to your skill development—physically, fundamentally, and mentally.

Identify players who you believe play the game within themselves, who do not try to do too much, who let the game come to them, who keep the game slow.

These players, most likely, have good understanding of themselves. Probably, they do not attempt to do things that they are not capable of. They typically have a sense of confidence and calm about them. They have a good level of personal awareness.

RISKS OF NOT BEING PERSONALLY AWARE

Naturally, there are risks that you take by not spending time getting to know yourself and not being honest about your strong points and limitations, on and off the baseball diamond. These personal risks include the following:

1. You can become indecisive about what you need to do to improve, since you have not taken the time to pinpoint important areas for your development.

2. You may have created a false sense of reality and security, since what you need to really work on to get better at has been overlooked and so it becomes easy to fool yourself.

3. You tend to mislead yourself by being too general and not specific enough about what you need to address so that you can improve your game.

Think of players—pitchers and position players—who do not seem to take time to get to know their strong points and limitations, who deny things about their shortcomings and who think that they are better than the facts suggest.

More often than not, these players are likely to be ones where the game speeds up on them, where they attempt to do too much, and to not play within the confines of their skill set.

BEING HONEST WITH YOURSELF

You may be familiar with the saying "honesty is the best policy". For the most part, this is a very sound saying and it is something that all of us can strive to attain.

Being honest about your skills, and the skills that you need to improve on, is useful for your development and success over the short term of the baseball season and the longer haul of your baseball career.

However, being honest with yourself as a baseball player is not an easy task. Baseball is a game of failure and it also is one of expectations. Playing baseball demands energy, effort, focus and a host of other mental qualities, besides talent and good fundamentals.

For players who work hard and want to succeed, it would be nice if everything went well. Considerable time and effort goes into the game. So, it is natural to want to see that things go well, even when the things that are happening are counter to what we expect. Trying to look away from failure and to see successes which are not there also is only natural.

These kinds of natural human tendencies are reasons why the mental domain of personal awareness is very important. Through the use of a very precise way of assessment of your skills—physical, fundamental, and mental—you can learn to accept what you need to work on and then commit to taking the steps to make adjustments, in order to get better.

THE SKILLS ASSESSMENT

The skills assessment will allow you to develop and improve your personal awareness.

The skills assessment is a process, in and of itself. It will allow you to make judgments about your strong points and limitations as a baseball player in the physical, mental, and fundamental domains.

From a skills assessment, you can use the resulting assessment information as a basis for putting together an individual development plan for yourself.

A skills assessment involves taking into account various sources of data about yourself. These data sources are:

1. Your own opinions about your strong points and limitations in the physical, fundamental, and mental domains.

2. The opinions of your coaches, instructors, teachers, and others.

3. Your baseball performance, as seen on video tape of your performances.

4. Any other relevant information that has to do with how you play the game

You can engage in a skills assessment by yourself. However, it is recommended that you involve one of your coaches in the skills assessment process, depending on your position.

You also can involve other individuals who know baseball and who are familiar with your development as a baseball player.

WHAT SKILLS SHOULD I ASSESS?

There are three sides to the game of baseball—the physical, fundamental, and mental.

You can choose to focus your skills assessment on all three of these domains or on one area only, such as the mental domain.

Table 6.1 illustrates examples of areas in which you can conduct a self-assessment of your skills and abilities that are related to baseball and your life.

TABLE 6.1. Some areas of the game of baseball that can be included in a skills assessment.

Area	Skills
Fundamental Assessment	• Hitting • Fielding • Throwing • Catching • Pitching • Running
Physical Assessment	• Strength • Flexibility • Quickness • Weight • Fitness
Mental Assessment	• Motivation • Confidence • Intensity • Focus • Composure • Self Esteem • Accountability

The advantage of a skills assessment is that you challenge yourself to be specific and honest about yourself, your game, and your life.

As a result, the time and energy spent on this assessment and the information that you get from assessment activities will enhance your personal awareness.

The information also can be used for formulating an individual development plan.

Steps in Conducting a Skills Assessment

There are many ways to guide yourself through an assessment of your strong points and limitations in various skill areas.

I will present a set of steps which have proven useful with major league and minor league players.

There are several steps involved in the skills assessment process. Although these steps will be presented in detail below, I want to just list them right here and then I will discuss them. The steps of the skills assessment process are:

1. Decide what domains to assess—the physical, fundamental, mental, or other areas. All of them, or only one or two of them.

2. For each domain that you choose, identify your current strong points in that area. A strong point is a skill in which you are solid, probably above average in relation to your competition.

3. Then, for the same area, identify your current limitations, that is, the skills that you need to get better at. A limitation is a skill that you need to improve on and that currently is an obstacle to getting better. If you can eliminate or minimize the limitation through hard work and dedicated practice, you are likely to become a better player and person.

4. Next, pinpoint your needs for development in that area, that is, the skills that you need to work on and that currently are limiting you.

5. Finally, review your skills assessment results with your coaches, in order to get their opinions and to see if they agree with you and then to formulate a player plan.

As you apply these steps, you are guiding yourself in gathering information about yourself to make decisions about yourself.

As part of the Complete Mental Game, a skills assessment is the process of gathering information about your strong points and limitations as a baseball player and as a person.

Figure 6.1 is a "Skills Assessment Form" which you can use as part of this process.

Figure 6.1: Example of a Skills Assessment Form.

Skills Assessment Form

Name:_____ Position:_____ Date: _____

Fundamentals

      Strong Points

      Limitations

Physical

      Strong Points

      Limitations

Mental

      Strong Points

      Limitations

Here are the steps of the skills assessment process in more detail.

Step 1: Decide What Domains You Want to Assess

There are three domains on which you can conduct a skills assessment—the physical domain, the fundamental domain, and the mental domain.

It is recommended that you select one to three domains. In doing so, make sure that you are clear with yourself about what you want to assess yourself on.

Here are the three domains and examples of things that may be relevant to you and your game and that you may want to assess:

- *Mental*—In this area, you can assess things like: how you prepare for competition, how mentally disciplined you are, how you compete, how you focus, how you balance baseball and school, and any other mental skills.

- *Physical*—In this area, you can assess things like your physical strength, quickness, nutrition, and other matters.

- *Fundamental*—In this area, you can assess the skills that have to do with your hitting, fielding, throwing, base running, or pitching , depending of course on your given position.

Make sure that you know why you have selected each of the domains and skills for assessment. Make sure that they are relevant to you and your overall game.

Step 2: Identify Your Current Strong Points

Once you have determined the domains for your skills assessment, proceed to identifying your current strong points in each of the areas.

In this regard, a strong point is a skill, quality, or attribute which you believe that you are very good at in relation to other players at your level of competition.

A strong point means that you consider yourself to be locked into the skill or ability, and that you are solid with it, most of the time.

You can focus this portion of your skills assessment by asking the question: *"What am I solid at that is a strong part of my game?"*

Here are examples of possible strong points for the mental domain:

1. I play the game with confidence. I do not back down.

2. I can keep myself on an even keel when things are not going my way on the field.

When you identify your strong points, discuss this information with your coaches. In addition, and possibly with their guidance, challenge yourself on why each one is a strong point.

Think about the reasons that you believe that each skill is a strong point: Is the skill a strong point because of my preparation? Is it due to my tenacity? Other reasons? Why do I do these things?

Table 6.2 displays examples of a set of strong points for two players based on this portion of his skills assessment.

TABLE 6.2. Examples of strong points of two baseball players as part of their skills assessment.

Pitcher: RHS	
Fundamental	• Pitch development; solid average slider with late bite • Consistent and sound delivery mechanics
Physical	• Arm Strength
Mental	• Mental discipline—following through on game plan
Position Player: 1B	
Fundamental	• Above average bat to ball ability
Physical	
Mental	• Composure—remains poised under pressure, especially when at bat with runners on base • Self-motivation—desire to improve overall game

Step 3: Identify Your Current Limitations

You now can proceed to identify skills and qualities in each domain that currently may be limiting your game. In this regard, a limitation is something—a lack of sufficient skill—that if you eliminate or minimize, you will become a more effective player.

You can focus this portion of your skills assessment by asking yourself the following question:

What do I need to improve at in this area so that I can become a better player?

Here are two examples of some possible limitations for the mental domain:

1. I get tentative delivering the pitch with men on base.

2. I become impatient when I have two strikes on me in the count.

For each limitation, challenge yourself as to why it is a limitation. In this regard, some challenging questions for the above two limitations are: Is it because I am not spending time on controlling the running game? Do I start thinking about getting hit rather than playing attention to the pitch?

Table 6.3 provides examples of a set of player limitations in the mental domain.

Table 6.3. Examples of limitations of two baseball players as part of their skills assessment.

Pitcher: RHS	
Fundamental	• Do not pitch inside with conviction • Controlling the running game; release time is high
Physical	
Mental	• Inconsistent attention on each pitch • Become frustrated with the uncontrollable

Position Player: OFR	
Fundamental	• Over aggressive swing, causing him to pull off the ball • Improper angles on fly balls
Physical	
Mental	

Step 4: Pinpoint Your Needs for Development

Once you have identified your strong points and limitations, go back to the list of limitations.

In conjunction with your coach, select two, three or four limitations which are most important to your development. These are your priority limitations. They are your needs for development.

Make sure that you know why you have selected these limitations. Then, begin thinking about what you can do in terms of drills and activities so that you can eliminate or minimize these limitations and, over the course of time, even make them strong points.

Step 5: Review Your Findings with Your Coach

Once you have completed your skills assessment, discuss with your coach the strong points, limitations, and developmental needs that you have come up with. Make sure that you are on the same page and in agreement with your coach and discuss any differences in his opinion with your findings.

Decide how you are going to address the limitations as part of a player plan or through other means.

The player plan will be discussed in the chapter about self-motivation and also in the chapter about mental discipline.

REFINING YOUR PERSONAL AWARENESS

As you proceed with your baseball career, strive to remain aware of yourself as a baseball player and as a person. Do not shortchange yourself in the personal awareness domain.

In addition to the skills assessment method described above, there are several ways in which you can "keep in contact" with yourself.

First, recognize that as you develop and as you proceed in the game of baseball, your strong points and limitations are going to change. This may happen because your role may change, or the level of competition may increase, or for other reasons. Whatever the case, continue to monitor yourself on your personal awareness of your development as a baseball player and as a person.

Second, make sure that you are accurate and honest in the self-assessment of your physical, fundamental, and mental skills.

Third, continue to discuss your development as a player—physically, fundamentally, and mentally—with coaches, instructors, and others who know your game.

Fourth, challenge yourself on what you are doing to improve your game, why you are doing these things, and how you are going to realize these accomplishments.

EXERCISES

1. Conduct a skills assessment on yourself. In addition, involve someone who knows you and your game to participate in the process. Use the resulting assessment information for your development.

2. Identify a player that you admire. List what you consider the player's strong points and limitations.

3. What are things about your development and performance that you tend to deny or not want to know about? Why do you feel this way? What is holding you back from being honest with yourself? How can you change this?

CHAPTER SEVEN

―――――― ✐ ――――――

SELF-MOTIVATION: SETTING AND PURSUING GOALS

Self-motivation is the third mental domain of the Complete Mental Game. Self-motivation is the mental domain which is at the heart of becoming and remaining a successful baseball player.

A baseball player who is self-motivated is usually considered by teammates, coaches, and opponents as being a competitor, no matter how much or how little natural talent that they possess. More often than not, the self-motivated player is described as someone who plays the game with a passion and enjoys himself in the process.

The self-motivated player does not require anyone standing over him, telling him what to do, and how to get better. Rather, he is committed to playing the game with enthusiasm and he is intent on pursuing and attaining goals.

The self-motivated player is at the ballpark early, working on his hitting, fielding, or pitching, depending on their role. He spends quality time in the weight room and maintains a good diet. He wants to get better mentally and emotionally, and he spends time working on these areas.

In contrast, a baseball player who is not self-motivated typically does not demonstrate a passion for the game. At best, this kind of player needs to be motivated by some other person or by something else such as by receiving attention from the media.

If a baseball player has to depend on other people or things to be motivated, he will probably not last long in the game, since baseball is a game where you fail more than succeed. This player, who is not self-motivated, usually will not play the game all out and he will not enjoy the process, since his motives are not coming from the inside—which is self-motivation.

Typically, baseball scouts and coaches comment about self-motivated players with various words and phrases. These include statements like playing the game with a passion; or noting in their reports that the player is a "baseball rat"; or that he likes to play for no other reason than that the game is there; or that nothing gets in the player's way of executing and getting the job done.

Self-motivation has to do with the setting and pursuing of goals that have to do with the physical, fundamental, and mental sides of the game. In this sense, self-motivation is an "inside mental and emotional job". The energy and enthusiasm comes from inside of the individual, not from the externals of the game.

Often, what baseball coaches, the media, and others observe on the field, and what they make judgments about, is the player and how he plays the game. When they do this, coaches and scouts actually are making judgments about are the player's motives, and his actions—his self-motivation.

Coaches and scouts are very concerned about how the player prepares, how he competes, how he goes about being a contributor to the team, and how he deals with his performance and makes adjustments. They are concerned about the motivation of the player.

Self-motivated players usually stand out. They play the game with a passion and pursue important goals.

TWO BASIC INGREDIENTS OF SELF-MOTIVATION
There are two basic ingredients which make up self-motivation. Both of these factors are under the control and influence of the player. These are:

1. *Motives:* What drives the player to play the game and to compete, day by day, game by game

2. *Actions*: How the player actually behaves—the actions that he takes—before the game, during it, and following the game

YOUR MOTIVES

The first basic ingredient of self-motivation involves your motives. In this respect, a motive is the reason and force that propels you to play the game. A motive provides meaning and drive for you, the player.

Some motives are internal like wanting to be the best that you can be on any given day, or attaining important goals that you have set for yourself and that will make you a better player.

Other motives, however, have an external stimulus such as getting recognized by the media, being selected to an all-star team, having people tell you how good you are, or making a lot of money.

The best motives for the player to be influenced by are the ones that are internal to him, those which come from his heart, so to speak. These are the longest lasting and they have the most staying power over the course of the season, especially when things are not going well on the field.

Without a motive that has meaning and that has built in drive, you will have little reason to execute as a hitter or pitcher, with dedication and with enthusiasm.

Internal motives can help you with the development and improvement of your game. Motives of this type will guide you to make sure that you are prepared to play and that you stay competitive throughout the contest

For example, your motives allow you to spend time in preparation for the coming season, especially when you would prefer to be doing other things. Motives are what drive you as you work out in the weight room or enable you to spend additional time in the batting cages.

Motives enable you to stay focused and in the moment and on your current at bat, despite the prior at bats which may have been poor ones.

Motives are thoughts and feelings that should excite you as you visualize yourself becoming a quality player. They allow you to never give up and to fight through things, especially when your performance is not what you expect.

YOUR ACTIONS

The second essential ingredient of self-motivation has to do with the actions which you take in support of your motives. Actions are the behaviors that need to occur in order to be motivated to play the game and to do it successfully.

The actions which you take as you play the game are driven by your motives. These actions, or behaviors, are linked to your overall game and determine how you prepare for competition, how you compete from pitch to pitch, and constructively deal with your performance.

Actions which are not purposefully linked to motives, though, will not be effective actions. Under these circumstances, you will be inefficient and ineffective, more often than not, if motives and action are not coordinated.

MOTIVES + ACTIONS = SELF-MOTIVATION

In essence, your self-motivation as a baseball player is composed of motives and actions, and these two ingredients need to be part of your mental game. This is why motivation is an inside job and why it is purposefully called, self-motivation, and not other-directed motivation.

When someone says that a baseball player is motivated to compete, what they are really referring to is that the player has a motive to compete *and* a way to act on this motive.

For example, a player can be considered as being self-motivated because he has a particular motive, such as engaging in each at bat to the best of his abilities. In addition, he engages in actions that are directed at the motive and which propel it, such as staying focused on each pitch and having a plan for the at bat.

If you are a self-motivated baseball player, then your motives and actions are under your direct influence, in coordination, and you want it that way.

Figure 7.1 illustrates the relationship between motivation + action, or motive for action, or motivation.

Figure 7.1: Relationship between motive and action.

WHEN TO CHECK YOURSELF OUT ABOUT SELF-MOTIVATION

You can review how you are doing in the self-motivation domain, at any time. However, the following time periods are good times to check yourself out in this area:

1. Before the season as a mental tune up so that you are prepared for spring training;

2. During the season at regularly scheduled times, such as every three weeks or every month; and

3. Any time when you feel that you are not playing the game with enthusiasm.

GOALS AND SELF-MOTIVATION

One of the most effective ways of making sure that you stay motivated to play baseball, day in and day out, is through the use of goals. Goals are how you make your motives real and meaningful and to which you can link specific actions and behaviors.

In all areas of human performance, including business and sport, there is considerable research about goals. Most of this research shows that people who have clear and realistic goals and who act on these goals with consistency and enthusiasm and specific actions are more likely to make progress toward and to attain their goals.

In baseball, the goals which a player sets for himself and that he willingly commits to follow are rooted in his motives. This relationship between motives and goals is what gives each goal its meaning.

Goals provide you with direction, enthusiasm, and a benchmark for monitoring your progress. Goals help you decide how you are going to develop as a player and improve your performance. Goals are your "reasons for being", both on and off the baseball diamond.

A goal is something that you want to accomplish that has meaning to you and your game. However, there are many types of goals which span across you as a baseball player and as a person.

Some types of goals are better for your self-motivation than other kinds. I will discuss the various types of goals, their advantages and disadvantages later in this chapter. Before we do that, however, let's take a look at your actions in relation to your goals.

ACTIONS IN RELATION TO GOALS

The actions, or behaviors, which you take to realize your goals as a baseball player are the means for making progress and for attaining goals. In this sense, the goal is the accomplishment or end product, while one's actions are the means to that accomplishment. You cannot have one without the other. If you do, your self-motivation will be short lived and incomplete.

When you set a goal for yourself, this accomplishment in and of itself will be a motivator for you. However, unless you follow through and act on the goal—with behaviors, drills, and exercises—you are limiting your chances in realizing the goal.

Personal actions are what contribute to the attainment of each of your goals. However, these actions cannot be left to chance. They have to be identified, specified, planned out, and monitored. Then, you must follow through with these actions and evaluate whether they are effective in attaining the goals. All of this involves self-motivation.

ADVANTAGES OF BEING SELF-MOTIVATED

There are advantages to being on the top of your game in the self-motivation domain. These are:

1. By being self-motivated, you provide yourself with an opportunity for having positive experiences, on and off the baseball diamond. You will be working toward accomplishments that are relevant and important to you, to your baseball success, and to your team. These pursuits, in and of themselves, are likely to be exciting and motivating.

2. Self-motivation enables you to know where you are headed in terms of your overall development as a baseball player and your daily performance. When you set and pursue goals with enthusiasm, you have some exciting benchmarks.

3. Self-motivation helps foster a sense of direction for your career and your game.

4. When you are motivated to take care of yourself, on and off the baseball diamond, you are able to minimize distractions and to focus on what is important in your game and your life.

DISADVANTAGES OF NOT BEING SELF-MOTIVATED

If you are not self-motivated to play baseball, you are running the risk of several things occurring. These are:

1. You will not enjoy the game since you are not being driven from within. It is hard enough to play without putting obstacles or lack of direction in your way.

2. Your competitiveness, energy, and effort will not be sustained, since your goals are not clear.

3. You will lack direction over the short term and longer haul of the season and perhaps your career.

4. You will lose interest in the game and your overall development as a baseball player. Things that were important to you may not be that important anymore.

Think of some players who you know or who you observed that you consider as being motivated to play baseball. These players may be position players or pitchers. What is it about those players that lead you to your conclusion about their motivation? What have you seen them say and do?

Now consider some players who you believe have not been self-motivated. What is it about their approach that leads you to believe this?

DEFINE SUCCESS IN WAYS THAT CAN MOTIVATE YOU

Playing baseball is not easy. It is easy, however, to get discouraged and to lose your self-motivation. You may start to question whether you are successful and you can get further discouraged.

To prevent this form of discouragement, one way of staying motivated is to define what success means to you. In terms of enhancing your self-motivation, you can start by defining success in ways which are controllable and which help place things in perspective.

Here is a definition of success that players have found helpful as they progress through minor league baseball up to and including the major leagues:

Success in baseball is the progressive realization of goals that are important to me and that are under my influence, both on and off the baseball diamond.

This definition of success has several features which can work for you. First, success is seen not as an end point but rather as process of getting better, one a step at a time. Second, the definition states that goals are accomplishments that are important to your development and your performance. Third, your version of success is focused on goals that are under your control and influence and not on things which are beyond your control and in the hands of others.

With this definition of success in baseball as an anchor point, you now can consider the many types of goals that you can set and pursue in baseball. As you will see, some of these types of goals are better to pursue than others.

DIFFERENTIATE THE TYPES OF GOALS WHICH CAN BE PURSUED

Goals can be considered as motives that the player is striving to attain. The attainment of goals requires action, enthusiasm, energy, and effort on your part.

Goals can be placed into categories, and some types of goals are better for you to set and pursue than other types.

1. *Outcome goals*: These are goals that have to do with the outcomes of your performance. Sometimes, these goals also are referred to as statistical goals. Examples of outcome goals are things like wins and losses, batting averages, hits allowed, and other kind of game statistics. Baseball outcomes, of course, are important to your success. They certainly are indicators which are used in evaluating your performance. However, outcome goals are not under your direct control and they are not the most desirable choices to use for goal setting. Many factors—players, weather conditions, umpires etc.—can influence the outcomes of playing baseball, not just you.

2. *Process goals*: These goals are ones that have to do with the process of playing the game and that relate to your performance and are under your control. Examples of process goals are: working the count during an at bat; catching balls in the dirt squarely as a catcher; using sound delivery

mechanics as a pitcher; putting up a quality at bat; following through on a five day routine; or other accomplishments that have to do with the process of playing the game. Process goals are very good goals on which to center your attention and your actions. They are goals which are more under your influence and control than outcome goals.

3. *Developmental goals*: These are goals that are very similar to process goals. However, developmental goals center on your development as a player, usually over the longer term, rather than for a game. When you state that you want to improve your focus while controlling the running game, you have set a developmental goal. Other examples of developmental goals have to do with accomplishments such as becoming physically stronger or increasingly confident. Developmental goals are good ones for you, since they are more directly under your control than outcome goals.

4. *Personal goals*: These are goals that have to do with accomplishments that you want to realize, off the baseball field. These goals have to do with how you want to be as a person or what personal areas that you want to develop and improve on. When you state that you want to be more considerate of your family, or that you want to complete all of your academic courses successfully for the school year you are dealing with personal goals. These kinds of goals are good ones to set, as long as you can influence their attainment through your actions.

Table 7.1 includes examples of outcome, process, developmental, and personal goals which have been set by professional baseball players.

Table 7.1. Examples of different types of goals set by professional baseball players.

Outcome Goals (not recommended)

- To have an earned run average under 3.00 for the season
- To hit 30 home runs

Process Goals

- To implement a consistent 5 day routine between starts
- To follow through with a plan for each of my at bats

Developmental Goals

- To develop a changeup that I can throw with consistency
- To learn how to play first base for this coming season

Personal goals

- To complete my last year of college
- To learn to speak Spanish

Set SMART Goals

Setting goals for your success as a baseball player begins with making sure that these goals are process, developmental, or personal in nature and that they are SMART.

In making this determination, the SMART approach has been found to be useful by players and staff.

In the Compete Mental Game, SMART refers to the steps involved in setting goals as a baseball player that will be self-motivating, over the short term and longer haul.

Here is how you can take a SMART approach to setting goals:

1. *Specific*—In order to attain a goal, it must be specific enough so that you know what you are working toward. Unless the goal is specific, you will not know if you are making progress toward it. When setting goals, you are encouraged to first make sure that each goal is a process, developmental, or personal goal…and then make it specific.

2. *Measurable*—When the goal has been specified, make sure that you have a way to measure, or monitor, the extent to which you are making progress toward it. There are many

ways to measure your progress toward a specific goal. These methods include: (a) your own judgment; (b) the evaluations of your coaches; (c) the effect that your progress toward the goal seems to be having on your performance; (d) the use of video; and (e) other methods.

3. *Attainable*—Make sure that the goal is one that you can attain in that it is one that is under your control. If you find that the goal is attainable, then proceed to the next goal setting step. If, however, you determine that you need to accomplish another more basic goal before you can work on the one you have set, then go back to step 1 above and specify that new goal.

4. *Relevant*—When you have specified the goal, determined a way to measure your progress on it, and the goal is considered to be an attainable one, it now is time to check whether the goal is relevant. In this sense, the goal is relevant if you can answer the following question: If I attain this goal, how will it make me a better player, or person? If I attain the goal, what will I be doing that I am not doing now? If you cannot answer these questions in the affirmative, then the goal may not be relevant and you should go back and decide why you set it.

5. *Time Framed*—If you have a goal that is specific, measurable, attainable, and relevant, now make sure that you know what time frame you are using to measure and evaluate your progress. This time frame may be at the end of the first half of the season, or at shorter intervals like every week, or following every start in the case of a pitcher.

Table 7.2 illustrates a variety of SMART goals for several position players and pitchers in various areas.

Table 7.2. Examples of SMART goals set by position players and pitchers.

Position Players—SMART Goals

- To develop an effective per game routine that I can implement, game by game, during the season
- To take a direct route when fielding balls during the game
- To improve my awareness and discipline of the strike zone

Pitchers—SMART Goals

- To develop and maintain a consistent rhythm, allowing for consistent release point and command
- To pay attention to the catcher and the glove when delivering pitches, one pitch at a time
- To consistently get through the front side on all pitches, allowing for consistent leverage and command of each pitch

Link Actions to Each SMART Goal

In order to enthusiastically pursue a SMART goal, you cannot just think about the goal or feel good about it. Although thinking about and feeling good about the goal may be important in having a positive mind set, you need to take specific and purposeful actions in order to make progress and to realize the goal.

Actions are the fuel that allows you to attain the goals. Purposeful actions are observable behaviors that are intended to help you attain a goal. These actions also may include thoughts and emotions that are directed at the goal.

Here are some guidelines to take in linking purposeful actions to a SMART goal:

1. Consider a range of actions to attain each goal. In this respect, use the VAK approach to make sure that you look at all options. The VAK approach allows you to consider a range of actions under the following categories:

    a. *Visual*: These include personal actions which involve your vision. Examples of these kinds of actions are: watching other players, reviewing videotape and the use of visualizing yourself attaining the goal.

    b. *Auditory:* These include personal actions which involve the use of your auditory or listening skills.

Examples are: listening to other players especially veteran ones and listening to audiotapes.

c. *Kinesthetic*: These are personal actions which include the physical or kinesthetic area such as physical practice, as well as other activities which have a physical element such as deep breathing and relaxation.

2. Make sure that the actions are specific enough so that you and other people who are working with you know what they are.

3. Inform other people such as another player or coach about how you plan to attain the goal. These are the actions that you need to take and implement.

4. Have a way to make sure that you are implementing the actions. This may be a checklist that you complete following each workout or writing down your follow through in a journal.

5. Recognize that you may have to adjust your actions, based on changes in the goal or the progress that you are making toward it.

6. Be aware of the roadblocks that may present themselves as you strive to attain each goal. Have a way to make sure that you can overcome any identified roadblocks.

Table 7.3 illustrates examples of purposeful actions that are linked to specific goals.

Table 7.3. Examples of purposeful actions that are linked to specific goals.

Position Player—Outfield Right

Goal	Actions
To improve awareness and discipline of the strike zone.	• Watch video of game at bats and discuss pitch selection and strike zone discipline with the hitting coach • Focus batting practice routine on swinging at strikes and centering the ball • Maintain use of hitting notebook during the season and discuss at bats with hitting coach

Pitcher—Left-handed Starter

Goal	Actions
To maintain consistent rhythm through the delivery allowing for consistent release points and command	• During bullpens, focus on increased tempo. Discuss with pitching coach afterwards • Watch video after each outing. Discuss with pitching coach • Dry delivery drills focusing on consistent rhythm • Review game video the day after each start and discuss with pitching coach

CONSTRUCT A PLAN TO SUSTAIN YOUR SELF-MOTIVATION

A plan is a way of accomplishing something. When the plan is constructed in step by step manner, it should help you to sustain your motivation.

Goals are the "what to accomplish", while activities constitute the "how to". Whenever you have set a goal, you should develop a plan. The plan should include the following components:

1. SMART Goal—"What I want to accomplish"

2. Plan activities—"How I will proceed to accomplish the goal"

3. Progress Evaluation—"How I will monitor my progress toward my goal"

Figure 7.2 is an example of a player plan for a minor league pitcher.

Figure 7.2: Example of Player Plan.

Strengths		
	Fundamental – Pitching	Pitch Development – Fastball (FB) has good sink
	Physical	Above Average Arm Strength
Limitations		
	Fundamental – Pitching	Delivery – Tendency to drift across body at descent
	Goal To drive w/backside and stay on line with a better finish	
Activities		Notes
Dry drills, glide to stride drills focusing on better direction (between starts)		
Two-ball drill for balance and separation (between starts)		
Watch game video after each outing and discuss direction and finish with pitching coach		
	Physical	Body Composition – High body fat percentage
	Goal To improve overall body composition by lowering fat mass	
Activities		Notes
Perform extra conditioning and cardio on off days		
Limit portion size at meals		
Improve food selection at meals through conversations with S&C staff		

Continued on next page

Mental	Composure – Does not remain poised and under emotional control as he develops his pitching skills
Goal To remain composed as he develops as a pitcher	

Activities	Notes
Yoga classes during Spring Training and Instructional league Reinforce him for making progress in his development and in separating his performance from himself as a person Teach the difference between his development and his immediate results (development is controllable; immediate results are not) Teach him to understand that his impatience is his own worst opponent (knowing himself is the key here) Use video to show when his composure on the mound is appropriate and inappropriate	Teach him to recognize when he begins to be impatient and to use breathing to calm himself down (MAC approach) ***M: Mind in the moment, focused on the current pitch to be delivered, take a deep breath ***A: Accept what is there in front of you, but do not judge it or do not judge yourself ***C: Commit to the pitch by throwing to and through the catcher and his glove.

The RWA Challenge

If you have set goals that are SMART and if you have a plan of activities for making progress toward their attainment, you can take the RWA challenge.

This is a way to test out, for yourself, your self-motivation to pursue the goals with enthusiasm. The RWA challenge encompasses three questions that you apply to each goal:

1. *Readiness*: Am I ready to work toward attainment of the goal?

2. *Willingness*: Am I willing to engage in the necessary actions to attain the goal?

3. *Ability*: Do I have the ability to follow through with a plan to attain the goal?

If the answers are yes to all three questions, your motivation is likely to be high. However, if the answer is no to one or more of these questions, you need to ask yourself why not yes and deal with your answer and make adjustments either in the goal, activities, or in other things.

EXERCISES

1. Identify a baseball player that you admire for his self-motivation. If possible, speak with that player. Discuss with him how he keeps himself motivated and what he does when his motivation dips, among other things.

2. Think about the times during the season that you find to be most difficult to motivate yourself. Why have these experiences occurred? What can you do in order to enhance your motivation when it is low?

3. What is your current vision for success in baseball? Give this some thought and then write a personal mission statement. Visualize yourself in relation to this personal mission statement. Set up a time period when you can see yourself in your mind succeeding at what you write about.

4. Maintain a diary or notebook about your experiences playing the game. Include your thoughts and feelings about these experiences. The use of a diary or journal will be covered in more detail later in the book.

CHAPTER EIGHT

———————— ⚾ ————————

MENTAL DISCIPLINE: HAVING A PLAN AND FOLLOWING IT

The purpose of this chapter is to describe and discuss mental discipline, which is the fourth mental domain of the Complete Mental Game. The information in this chapter will help you to decide how to be effectively disciplined, mentally and emotionally, so that you can take charge of and focus on the process of playing baseball.

I want to begin this chapter by challenging you to appreciate the importance of having a plan and willingness to follow through with one. Having a plan and following it is the essence of being mentally disciplined.

In terms of your mental discipline, I want you to learn to develop a solid way to prepare for each game, a plan that you can take into the game, and a plan for your longer range development.

Playing baseball successfully requires various kind of plans, long range ones and game plans, and all effective plans require mental discipline.

Mental discipline is a very special state of mind and habit. If you can develop and refine your mental discipline, you will be prepared for just about any situation during the season and over the course of your career in the game.

Mental discipline is reflected in how you manage yourself and your plan—the goals and actions that you take so that you can be successful. Mental discipline is relevant to you and your success before the game, during it, and after the game.

The need for mental discipline escapes no one, whatever your role and position on the team.

Mental discipline includes planning out how you are going to accomplish your goals and then how you are going to follow through on your plan in terms of specific actions.

Mental discipline also involves how you deal with your time off the field. It includes how you relate to people, places, and things as well as how you deal with adverse situations such as physical injuries and working through any physical rehabilitation that you may experience.

QUALITIES OF MENTAL DISCIPLINE

Mental discipline contributes to and enhances the quality of your preparation—not just mentally and emotionally—but also in the physical and fundamental areas.

There are three important psychological indicators of mental discipline. As part of the Compete Mental Game, they are referred to as the three Ps: Patience, Persistence, and Perseverance.

1. *Patience*: This is your willingness to take the time to attain your goals, on and off the baseball diamond, even if that takes longer than expected, such as learning a new pitch, or learning to be more disciplined at the plate. Patience requires that you make sure you know what each goal is and what it entails on your part in order to attain it. Patience is needed to attain any number of goals in baseball, like striving to make it to the major leagues, or having consistent quality starts, or making progress in coming back from surgery.

2. *Persistence*: This is making a conscious decision to never give up. It also can be termed as refusal to quit. Persistence can be seen in working relentlessly to pursue your goals and working on them, no matter how long it takes.

3. *Perseverance*: This has to do with being able to stay the course in the pursuit of your goals, in spite of roadblocks and setbacks which you may encounter along the way. Persistence reflects learning from your failures and applying what you have learned from these experiences so that you can make adjustments and get better.

Whatever the case, however, all baseball players, yourself included, are urged to take stock of their mental discipline and to be able to develop, refine, or maintain it.

BASEBALL AND LIFE REQUIRE MENTAL DISCIPLINE

Mental discipline, or the lack of it, can make or break your baseball career and other aspects of your life. Mental discipline affects how you function as a baseball player and as a person in a range of areas. Some of these areas are:

- What you do with your life and with whom you associate at home, in the hotel, or at school, before you come to the ballpark

- What kind of routines you implement, as you arrive in the clubhouse and as you get ready for the game

- What you do on the field, just prior to the game, for batting and fielding practice

- How you keep your mind in the moment and weed out distractions, pitch to pitch, as the game begins and as it proceeds

- The extent to which you take the time to review your performance, post-game, in a step by step and accurate manner

More specifically, mental discipline requires that you acquire a personal handle on the following:

- Having a planned and purposeful pre game routine and following through with it

- Knowing what you want to accomplish for the game, including having a specific game plan for it

- Managing yourself to follow through on your game plan

- Making adjustments within the framework of your game plan

- Being patient, persistent, and persevering in spite of setbacks and adversity

To be able to say that you are mentally disciplined as a baseball player is to say that your coaches and teammates can count on you because of the following reasons:

- You are pursuing SMART goals

- You have a plan for attaining these goals

- You are willing to follow through on the plan

- You use accurate feedback from game performance to make adjustments to your plan

ADVANTAGES OF MENTAL DISCIPLINE

There are many advantages to your game and life that come with being mentally disciplined. These advantages are:

1. You will be able to effectively manage your thoughts, emotions, and actions, which will help you to be confident with your approach to playing the game.

2. You can easily keep your mind set on specific things, which keeps you from rushing into things and making mistakes.

3. You will be aware of what you will be doing, pitch by pitch as well as at other times during the day.

4. You are likely to feel better about yourself, since you will have put in the work to plan what you are going to accomplish and how you are going to proceed, prior to doing it.

Think of players who you believe are disciplined players. What is it about these players that you admire?

Risks of Not Being Mentally Disciplined

If you are not mentally disciplined, however, you are more than likely to incur several personal risks. These risks are:

1. You are likely to be inconsistent in your performance, due to poor pre game preparation or a vague game plan.

2. You can very easily neglect to follow through with your good intentions, since there is no reference point on which to center your attention.

3. You could feel frustrated and lose your willingness to compete.

4. You can spend considerable time in changing or tinkering with your routine, or about how to approach your at bats, or how to attack hitters.

Think of players who are not disciplined in terms of their routines and actions. What do they display which leads you to this judgment?

Developing and Refining Your Mental Discipline

Developing and refining your mental discipline as a baseball player is important to your career, over the short term and longer term.

Major league baseball players and others who have been successful at playing the game have identified a range of tasks to which mental discipline is relevant.

These tasks deal with your mental discipline, both on and off the baseball diamond and they have to do with you as a performer and as a player.

Consider the following tasks with respect to mental discipline:

1. Managing your time

2. Dealing with procrastination

3. Implementing a pre-game routine

4. Firming up a starting pitcher's five day routine

5. Making sure about a relief pitcher's routine

6. Developing and following through with a game plan

7. Coping with risk -- people, places, and things

8. Working through physical injury and rehabilitation

Each one of these tasks will now be discussed in relation to the mental domain of mental discipline.

Managing Your Time

Time is a resource that is available to you as a baseball player and as a person. It is there in front of you, for your use.

There is only a certain amount of time which is available to you for baseball. You only have so much time to get ready to compete, for getting the job done in the moment, once the game begins, as well as throughout the baseball season.

In addition, time is available for you to get involved in other things which reflect your core personal values like being with your family, continuing your education, and other areas of your life.

How you use your time is an important task, on and off the baseball diamond—daily, weekly, and for longer time intervals.

In terms of your mental discipline and the quality of your preparation, the management of your time is essential for your success. For the most part, baseball players who are good time managers are typically good performers.

Time management is the process of recognizing the amount of time that you have at your disposal and then allocating that time to your priorities and tasks.

The effective management of your time in baseball and beyond can be enhanced by reliance on the following guidelines:

1. *Get your priorities clear*—Make sure that you are clear as to your priorities, especially during the season. These priorities should encompass playing baseball in coordination with living your life. Unless you recognize what are the most important things to you—your priorities—there will be no reference point about how to use your time. Once you get to the ballpark, you have priorities such as getting ready to play and being willing to compete, one pitch at a time. Once you

leave the ballpark, you have other priorities like spending quality time with your family.

2. *Identify your baseball activities*—As a baseball player, decide what activities you need to spend your time on and when. In this sense, be clear about what you need to spend time on, before the game, during the game, and when the game is over. During the off season, decide what you need to spend time on so that you can develop your game and get better at it. Make a list of those activities and then monitor yourself on the use of your time in relation to them. Be honest when you evaluate yourself about time spent on your baseball activities

3. *Pinpoint your life commitments*—For other areas of your life beyond baseball such as school, families, and friends, decide what activities are important and how much time you need to devote to them. Make sure that you are not over-spending or under-spending your time. Make sure that these commitments mesh with your core values. Here too, be honest and make adjustments in your commitments, as may be necessary.

4. *Put it on paper*—Maintain a notebook or calendar for recording your most important activities for both baseball and non-baseball areas. Then, evaluate yourself on these activities. Are you spending sufficient time on each activity; too much time; not enough time? Based on your evaluations, make adjustments in how you use your time accordingly as a baseball player and as a person.

DEALING WITH PROCRASTINATION

Putting things off can put a damper on your baseball performance and your career. Not doing the things that are necessary for your development and your performance as a baseball player can quickly place you "behind the eight ball".

Procrastination is an indicator of poor mental discipline. It is the mental habit of putting things off that you want to do; sometimes these are things which you are committed to as a baseball player. Procrastination can put a damper on your success in baseball.

If, for example, you want to develop your upper body strength and you put off spending time on this in the weight room, you are engaged in procrastination.

If you are committed to improving your slider and you put off working on it as part of your bullpen sessions, you are involved with procrastination.

You can use mental discipline in preventing and dealing with your tendencies to procrastinate, both on and off the baseball diamond. Here are some guidelines that you can consider:

1. *Confront your tendencies*—Identify the areas as a baseball player in which you tend to procrastinate. This may be areas like working on your mental game, or perhaps the area has to do with implementing a more effective pre game routine. Maybe, the area of procrastination is about not improving your eating habits or some other aspect of your physical development, like not setting up a conditioning plan for the season.

2. *Understand why*—For each area, in which you tend to procrastinate, identify the possible reasons for these tendencies. Why do you let things go? Are you fearful of failure? Why do you procrastinate? Are you concerned with what others may think?

3. *Challenge yourself*—When you are able to identify the reasons for your procrastination, challenge yourself to reframe your thoughts. Recognize that by putting things off (procrastination) you are limiting your development and career. Make it a point to follow through, to let your behaviors get the job done.

4. *Be preventive*—Remain alert to the people, places, and things about which you tend to procrastinate and then make sure that you have a way of not letting procrastination occur.

IMPLEMENTING A PRE-GAME ROUTINE

The time before the game is very important for the quality of your preparation. This is the case, no matter what position you play or whether you are a starting pitcher or a reliever.

Without doubt, your mental discipline is important during pre-game time.

The development and implementation of a pre-game routine is the foundation of this time period and mental discipline is a key ingredient here.

A pre-game routine is really a plan for how you use your time before the game. This routine can include the time when you arrive at the ballpark, but it also can include the time before you get there.

An effective pre game routine is designed to get you ready to compete for the game. This readiness involves mental discipline.

The following guidelines can help the development of an effective pre game routine:

1. *Put things in blocks*—Divide the pre-game time period up into time blocks. These time blocks may include ones like the following: (a) arriving at the park and getting dressed in the locker room; (b) work in the batting cages or the bullpen; (c) participation in weight room activities; (d) spending time on the field including batting practice; (e) relaxing; (f) engaging in some mental work such as visualization; and (g) getting ready to take the field.

2. *Decide what you want*—For each time block, decide what you are going to accomplish—these are your process goals for that period. For example, if you are working in the batting cages, what do you want to accomplish during that time? During on the field batting practice, what are you working on?

3. *Know how to proceed*—For the things that you are going to accomplish, you can decide how you are going to realize them. These are your pre game activities for each accomplishment.

4. *Keep accountable*—Decide that you will monitor yourself on your time blocks. You want to evaluate yourself on the

extent to which you have followed through on each time block.

You can write down your pre game routine and use it to help you get ready for each game. You can post it in your locker.

This does not have to be very detailed. It just must be sufficient to keep you focused on what you expect to accomplish before the game and how you go about doing that.

Table 8.1 provides examples of pre-game routines for some players.

TABLE 8.1. Examples of pre-game routines of baseball players.

Catcher

- Arrive at the Ballpark
- Lunch
- Go through mail and requests
- Cardio work
- Hit in cages
- Relax, play chess
- Batting practice
- Meet with pitching coach and starting pitcher
- Snack
- Dressed for game
- Bullpen
- Game

Infielder

- Arrive at ballpark
- Weight room
- Lunch
- Hit off the ground balls during batting practice
- Take batting practice
- Use video to review opposing pitcher
- Ready for game
- Game time

FIRMING UP A STARTING PITCHER'S FIVE DAY ROUTINE

Another aspect of baseball performance in which mental discipline is necessary is the days between outings for starting pitchers.

Almost all major league starting pitchers are scheduled to pitch every five days. For instance, if a starting pitcher's last outing was on a Tuesday, his next start will be on the coming Sunday. The five days between his last outing and the upcoming one are days when mental discipline is crucial.

A starting pitcher's five day routine needs to be developed with a plan and the pitcher needs to be disciplined in following through on this routine.

Without a plan for these five days, the pitcher is setting the conditions for a poor outing.

If you are a starting pitcher, firming up your five day routine requires that specific attention be given by you and your pitching coach to the following kinds of decisions:

1. When you will throw your bullpen/side session and what will you work on during that time.

2. When you will engage in your physical work including cardio and strength work, and what will the work consist of.

3. When you will review your recent outing and get prepared for the next one using video

4. Other activities.

Table 8.2 is an example of a planned five day routine of a major league pitcher.

TABLE 8.2. Example of a 5-day routine for a starting pitcher

Day 1 (day following outing)	• Review performance with pitching coach • Cardio and flexibility work • Shag in outfield during batting practice
Day 2	• Running • Watch video of recent outing (assessment) • Throwing program (light)
Day 3	• Bullpen session • Review bullpen with pitching coach • Shag during batting practice

Day 4	• Review opposing lineup for next start (video review, discussion with pitching coach) • Cardio and stretching
Day 5 (day of start)	• Light stretching • Light lunch/dinner • Mental preparation • Meeting with pitching coach and catcher • Relax • Pre-game bullpen • Game

Planning out a five day routine is important for any starting pitcher. What is equally important, though, is for the pitcher to follow through on the routine.

It makes little sense to have an outline on paper but to not implement it with consistency or in accord with high standards.

The follow through with the routine is what mental discipline is about.

If you are a starting pitcher, here are some questions that you can ask yourself that are intended to help you follow through on your five day routine:

1. What are the activities which constitute my five day routine?

2. Have I implemented each of these activities between my starts?

3. Have I engaged in each of these activities with quality effort?

4. What obstacles, if any, did I encounter in following through?

5. How can I improve my five day routine including my follow through with it?

Making Sure about a Relief Pitcher's Routine

Relief pitchers, too, also require mental discipline in order to prepare for their appearances.

However, pitchers who come out of the bullpen in relief of another pitcher do not know for sure whether they will be called into the game or exactly when that will be.

Given this uncertainty of getting in the game, the relief pitcher will benefit from having a way to get mentally ready and physically ready.

The routine of a relief pitcher can include the following steps, all of which require mental discipline:

1. Watching the game from the bullpen and noting what the lineup is doing against the current pitcher.

2. Using visualization and relaxation to calm the mind before he begins to warm up.

3. Engaging in the warm up with the expectation that you will be going into the game, if you get the call.

4. Going back to step no. 1 above, if you warm up and do not go into the game.

The relief pitcher also needs to monitor himself on his bullpen routine and make sure that he is implementing it as intended.

Developing and Following Through with a Game Plan

Each game is an event unto itself. When the previous game is over, a new one will begin, in due course, possibly the next day. The quality of your preparation for one game can effectively stem from what you have learned about yourself from the prior contest.

However, a game plan must be linked to the upcoming game, not what has already happened. Adjustments in a game plan need to be made, depending on the upcoming opponent.

Mental discipline is at the basis of an effective game plan, from firming it up to being able to follow through with it.

A game plan can be considered the approach that you will take so that you can be effective in a particular game. Your game plan includes what you want to accomplish in game and how you will go about doing this.

A game plan should be based on your current strengths and limitations as a baseball player.

You can construct a game plan for your offense (hitting) and for your defense, if you are a position player. If you are a starting pitcher, you can have a game plan for the opponent whom you will face in your upcoming start.

In terms of mental discipline, the following factors need to be considered in developing an effective game plan:

1. Make sure that you are aware of your strong points and limitations, given your role and given the opponent.

2. Challenge yourself about your willingness to commit to being prepared for the game.

3. Obtain an understanding of the opponent including the pitcher that you will be facing if you are a position player; or the lineup that you will be facing if you are a pitcher.

4. Decide what you want to accomplish against this opponent and make sure that these are things which are under your influence. For example, what do you expect to do in each of your at bats? What do you expect to do with your pitches?

5. Clarify with yourself and your coaches how you are going to realize these accomplishments.

6. Commit to following through on your game plan.

7. Evaluate whether and to what extent you have followed your game plan. If you have followed your plan, you can evaluate how effective the plan was. If you did not follow through with your plan, you need to identify why you did not implement it.

Table 8.3 includes example game plans from some professional baseball players.

TABLE 8.3. Example of game plans for some baseball players

Position Player	• Stay inside the ball on this pitcher • Pay attention to the ball • Make solid contact with my pitches • Let go of my at bats
Pitcher	• Command of my fastball • Work with good tempo • Control the running game • Mind in the moment

COPING WITH RISK—PEOPLE, PLACES, THINGS

Like most professional athletes and many amateur ones as well, baseball players exist in a high risk environment. Here, we are talking about psychological risk and physical risk. In this regard, risk that exists in the environment, and the consequences that go along with them, are part and parcel with playing the game.

Risk as a baseball player has to do with the likelihood that you can become influenced by people, places, and things that will do you no good.

The domain of mental discipline is an important area for coping effectively with risk.

You can minimize the risks that are present in your immediate environment by using a mentally disciplined approach. In that regard, here are guidelines to follow:

1. *Know your environments*—Identify the personal environments in which you function on a daily basis and at other times as part of your involvement in baseball. These environments may include the following: school, home, on the road, clubhouse, or other settings.

2. *Pinpoint the people*—In terms of these environments, identify the types of people who could pull you in the wrong direction, if you were to decide that you wanted to go that way. These people might include the following types: gamblers, drug dealers, acquaintances, or others.

3. *Be aware of the places*—Clarify the kinds of places that place you at risk and that you want to avoid or have a plan for being in them. These places could include the following:

bars and clubs, hotel rooms and lounges, gambling casinos, and other places.

4.   *Things to avoid*—Review all of the things that can put you at risk. In particular, consider the range of substances that may be available to you in your role as a baseball player. These could be alcohol, drugs of abuse, steroids, amphetamines, and other substances. Educate yourself on how these substances can place you at risk and exercise your mental discipline in not using them.

WORKING THROUGH PHYSICAL INJURY AND REHABILITATION

Physical injury is a fact of life in playing sports including baseball. It is possible that you have had one or more physical injuries that have kept you out of the game for a period of time. For some of you, that period of time may have been months, even longer.

The task of going through physical rehabilitation is not an easy matter. It is a challenging and frustrating time period for you and others. In order to cope effectively with physical injury and the physical rehabilitation which often accompanies it, mental discipline is required.

As we have been discussing throughout this chapter, mental discipline means your willingness to have a plan and follow through with it.

Here is a set of mental discipline guidelines for helping you cope with physical injury and rehabilitation:

1.   Take your physical rehabilitation one day at a time. Consider each session with the strength coach or physical therapist as a mini-game.

2.   Look for the "small wins" for every session. Acknowledge the grind but look for things that you have accomplished, no matter how small they may be.

3.   Communicate with the individual who is responsible for your physical rehabilitation. Work with that individual so that you know what are the long term and short term goals as well as the activities.

4. If you do not understand any aspect of the rehabilitation plan ask questions. Do not let this go by the wayside. The more that you know what your plan consists of, the more you will be able to engage yourself in it.

5. Monitor the quality and quantity of your effort during all rehab sessions including your attitude. Toward that end, here are some self-evaluation questions:

   a. Did I begin my session on time?

   b. Was I actively engaged in the session or did I cut some corners?

   c. Did I complete all of the exercises and activities?

   d. What were my small wins for this session?

EXERCISES

1. Divide up the calendar year into the following phases: (a) spring training, (b) baseball season, (c) fall/winter ball, and (d) off season. Then, for each phase, identify the activities that you need to follow through on during these time periods. Next, decide how you are going to monitor yourself and follow through on them.

2. Decide what kinds of plans you need to have so that you can get the most out of your potential as a baseball player. Examples of these plans may include ones such as the following: (a) pre game routine, (b) plan for the days between your starts if a starting pitcher, (c) game plan, (d) plan for your off season continuing, and (e) other kind of plan. For each kind of plan that you have selected, write down the following:

   a. What do you expect to accomplish with that kind of plan?

     b.   What activities will be part of the plan?

     c.   How will you monitor yourself on it?

4.   Identify some baseball players who you consider to be models of good mental discipline. Why did you choose those players? What are the behaviors that led you to these choices? How can you incorporate these qualities into your own mental game? If possible, meet with these players and discuss their attitude and approach to mental discipline.

5.   What are factors in your life and immediate environment that could prevent you from being effectively self-disciplined? In this respect, identify any relevant PPTs—People, Places, and Things.

6.   Who comprises your support system? Why can you trust these people? How can you rely on them?

PART THREE

COMPETITIVE FOLLOW THROUGH:
BEING IN THE MOMENT

CHAPTER NINE

―――――― 🏐 ――――――

SELF-CONFIDENCE: BELIEVING IN YOUR CAPACITY TO COMPETE

The purpose of this chapter is to present information about the mental domain of self-confidence, which is the fifth mental domain of the Complete Mental Game.

In this chapter, you will be provided guidelines about how to develop your self-confidence as a baseball player, as well as how to regain self-confidence when it becomes inconsistent and you do not feel confident.

The development and maintenance of your self-confidence is an important part of the Complete Mental Game. As a baseball player, you cannot afford to leave the development and maintenance of your self-confidence to chance. If you do not believe in yourself as a hitter, fielder, or pitcher, then you need to pay attention to how to improve confidence which you have in your skills and abilities.

If you neglect the mental domain of self-confidence, then your overall development as a player can be stymied. In addition, your day to day performance will be minimized. A neglect of your self-confidence as a baseball player even can lead to low feelings about yourself and your abilities outside of baseball.

Self-confidence is an area that you need to pay attention to on a routine basis—during spring training, as part of the actual baseball season, and once the season is concluded.

As one of the 12 mental domains of the Complete Mental Game, self-confidence has to do with the belief that you have in your capacity to compete—that you can hit, throw, field, run the bases, or pitch, depending on your role.

More specifically, self-confidence reflects the belief that you have in your skills and abilities to realize successful performance outcomes by taking charge of the process of playing the game.

Self-confidence also has longer range aspects since it pertains to your belief in having a successful career outside of baseball, when the game over for you.

Although I will be discussing self-confidence as it pertains to baseball, self-confidence also is essential to other aspects of your life, off the baseball diamond.

Two Dimensions of Self-Confidence

There are two psychological dimensions of self-confidence. Both dimensions are important to your development and your performance as a baseball player.

The first dimension involves self-confidence as a human trait. This is your natural tendency, no matter what you are doing, to believe in yourself and your capacity to compete.

As a human trait, self-confidence means that you believe in your skills and abilities as a baseball player to compete and to get the job done—to succeed in playing the game so that the opposition notices you and has to take you into account.

The second dimension of self-confidence is referred to as situation specific self-confidence. In this respect, there are certain situations during the course of a game where your confidence will vary; it will go up or down. During one at bat, you may feel confident, but you may lose your confidence during the next at bat and that lack of self-confidence may carry over through the rest of the game.

There also are times when you start out the game not really feeling confident, but your confidence strengthens as the game proceeds. If, for example, a pitcher does not have command of his pitches during the first inning or two of the game, his confidence may be low. However, if he then is able to adjust and now he can locate his pitches and throw strikes, his confidence is likely to go up.

Self-confidence means that you believe that you are able to play the game effectively, that you have the capacity to compete. It means you have a belief that you will execute, that you will get the job done as you "cross the lines", from pitch to pitch throughout the course of the game.

Over the longer haul, self-confidence also means that you believe that you will have a good career and attain your long term goals.

MIND SET FOR SELF-CONFIDENCE

A baseball player, including you, is not entitled to be self-confident. You do not become and remain confident by simply showing up to the ballpark, or by just being present on the field. Rather, you have to earn the confidence which you have in yourself and how you play the game.

The task of being a self-confident baseball player becomes more effective and efficient, however, if you know how to set your mind in a way that will foster self-confidence.

You can acquire and develop self-confidence by committing to the quality of your preparation, particularly the quality of your practice sessions and pre game routines. In addition, self-confidence is bolstered by being willing to deal, head on, with the ups and downs of playing the game.

Through a proper mind set for self-confidence, you will provide a boost to the belief which you have in yourself and how you play the game.

In terms of being self-confident, though, you do not want to devalue yourself, that is, to put yourself down. Rather, you want a mindset that will allow you to be honest with yourself about your skills and abilities. You want to be comfortable with facing your performances and your results—straight on and honestly—whether they are good or not so good.

Self-confidence, however, is not to be equated with other states, such as the one termed cockiness. Self-confidence comes from being prepared for the season and for the game as well as from being honest about yourself and respecting the game. In contrast, cockiness comes from not really being sure of yourself, but denying that you have work to do on your game.

ADVANTAGES OF BEING SELF-CONFIDENT

There are many reasons why being self-confident will enhance your performance as a baseball player.

First, when you are self-confident, you will enjoy the process of playing the game more than if you were not confident in your abilities. This sense of enjoyment is likely to be present in you if you have prepared yourself to play. With a sense of preparedness, it is easier to get into the game and not to question how you play, make decisions, make adjustments, and compete from pitch to pitch.

Second, you will perform more effectively when you are self-confident. Your mind will be quicker, enabling you to stay focused on the task at hand and in the moment. Consequently, you will be less likely to drift into feelings of not being able to execute. In essence, when you are confident of your abilities as a baseball player, you are focused on the process of playing the game and you are not concerned about failing. A focus on outcomes can limit self-confidence, since your mind is not on things under your control. You are thinking about results and other things you cannot control.

Third, with self-confidence, you will want to continue to stretch yourself and improve your overall game. This is because you have not left your self-confidence to chance. You see baseball not only as a process but as something in which you are in continuous improvement.

Think of players who you believe have been confident in how they have played the game. How have these players looked? How have they carried themselves as performers? What about their body language. What did they say and do?

It is accurate to say that these players were not simply born that way. There is most likely a mind set about their game. They have not taken self-confidence as an entitlement. Rather, they have worked hard at being confident.

These players most likely have used some of the approaches that we will discuss in subsequent sections of this chapter.

DISADVANTAGES OF NOT BEING SELF-CONFIDENT

When you are not confident about yourself and your abilities to play the game of baseball, however, a number of thoughts, emotions, and actions are likely to be present.

First, you will feel inclined not to trust your abilities as a baseball player. This type of feeling creates doubt about your skills and abilities, doubts that you will not get the job done. You question what you are doing. You worry. You tend to avoid situations like pitching inside, or making solid contact with off speed pitches.

Second, when you are not self-confident, you will be reluctant to take the ball, if you are a pitcher or you will be tentative to proceed with an at bat, or with making the play on defense. This will be the case especially in demanding and pressure game situations, when the game is on the line.

Third, you will come across to the opposition as being tentative and timid, rather than being aggressive with how you play the game. Your body language will be poor.

Fourth, without a self-confident mind set, you will tend to be overly conscious of specific game situations, since the attention is likely to be on you. In this respect, you will not enjoy playing. Rather, you will be concerned about what others are thinking about you. Your consciousness of yourself will tend to be magnified.

Think of players who have not appeared to be self-confident. How are these players different than players who have been confident? How do you think that they got that way?

DEVELOPING AND MAINTAINING YOUR SELF-CONFIDENCE

You can influence the development of your self-confidence and also strive to maintain it, game by game, as well as throughout the season. The task of being able to develop and maintain self-confidence is under your control and influence.

Here are guidelines that you can use to develop and maintain your self-confidence:

1. Distinguish self-confidence from cockiness

2. Make sense of self-confidence and your results

3. Assess your self-confidence

4. Use goals to enhance your self-confidence

5. Visualize being self-confident

6. Employ affirmations that influence your self-confidence

7. Demonstrate confident body language

8. Engage in purposeful practice

9. Monitor your self-confidence

Each one of these guidelines now will be discussed.

DISTINGUISH SELF-CONFIDENCE FROM COCKINESS

In order to develop and maintain your self-confidence, it is important to distinguish between being self-confident and being cocky.

Self-confidence is the belief that you have in your capacity to compete, to play the game of baseball, to have an effect on the opponent. In essence, self-confidence has to do with trusting yourself. It also has to do with being humble and not thinking too much of yourself, of not getting a big head.

Players, who are self-confident, typically respect the game and they are considerate of others. These players prepare to compete, play the game hard, and are humble about their accomplishments.

Cockiness is exhibited by players who may not be self-confident. A player who is cocky may be talented. However, the cocky player may really be insecure about his abilities and covers this with an air of bravado.

A cocky player may say and do things that he thinks gives the impression of being confident and in control of his game. A cocky player may only be deceiving himself, about himself.

As you play the game, keep in touch with yourself about your motives and mind set. If you find yourself starting to be cocky, make it a point to step back and ask yourself what is occurring that is creating a cocky attitude in you.

If you find yourself starting to get cocky, this is a time for an honest confronting of yourself. It is a time for readjustment of your mind set back to a confident player and person.

MAKE SENSE OF SELF-CONFIDENCE AND YOUR RESULTS

Which came first, the chicken or the egg? This is a phrase that has long been used to discuss situations that are not clear as to what caused what.

The same kind of phrase can be applied to your self-confidence: What comes first, your self-confidence which contributes to your results or do your results dictate your self-confidence?

I recommend strongly that you do not spend time trying to prove which one—self-confidence or results—lead to the other, since both ways are necessary to be a successful baseball player. Self-confidence contributes to your results and when you obtain good results, you bolster your self-confidence.

In this respect, it is recommended that you understand what self-confidence is and how to develop and maintain it, while recognizing when you are losing it. An important initial step here is conducting an assessment of your self-confidence.

ASSESS YOUR SELF-CONFIDENCE

One of the initial steps in developing and maintaining self-confidence is to get a handle, or read, on how confident you are as a baseball player, both overall in terms of your career as well as in terms of specific aspects of your game.

The best way to accomplish this is to conduct an assessment of your self-confidence. You can do this by considering several areas that have to do with self-confidence and some questions that pertain to each area.

In responding to these areas and questions, consider self-confidence as the following: The belief that you have in your abilities to execute and perform effectively in your role as a baseball player and with respect your position on the team.

1. *Determine my feelings about being successful playing the game of baseball.* How confident am I at this time in terms of playing baseball? What discourages me from wanting to continue to play the game? What encourages me?

2. *Pinpoint the times when I am most confident.* When is my confidence very solid as a baseball player? What are specific types of game and game situations when I believe that I will succeed?

3. *Identify the derailers of my confidence.* What are factors that cause me to lose my confidence? What are types of games and game situations when I have lost my confidence?

4. *Know how I react to my self-confidence.* When I lose confidence in myself as a baseball player, what do I do to regroup and to regain my confidence? When do I have the most difficulty in regaining self-confidence?

Your consideration of these areas will result in some specific information. Through this assessment process, you should learn such things as: (a) how encouraged or discouraged you are at the moment in terms of your career, (b) the factors and times which enhance your confidence, (c) the things which delimit it, and (d) how you react when your confidence is down.

This information can be used to decide what areas you need to continue to be aware of and possibly do some work.

USE GOALS TO ENHANCE YOUR SELF-CONFIDENCE

In Chapter 3, I discussed the importance of developmental and process goals for self-motivation. As you may recall, goals are the motives for your actions, on and off the baseball diamond.

Developmental and process goals are also useful for enhancing your self-confidence. When you have set goals that relate to your development and the process of playing the game, and when you work at attaining these goals, self-confidence can be increased.

The reason for this is that goals provide a structure and a focus for your preparation. Goals allow you to become confident that you will achieve them.

For each and every goal that you have set for yourself as a baseball player, check yourself out on the following:

1. Recognize the relevance of each goal that you have set and give yourself credit that you have set the goal.

2. Develop a feeling that you will make progress and attain the goal.

3. Expect that, by following through with dedicated work and practice, you will make progress toward the goal. Reinforce yourself in following through with practice that is dedicated to the goal.

VISUALIZE BEING SELF-CONFIDENT

The use of your visual senses can be helpful in developing and maintaining self-confidence in your game. When you visualize something being accomplished, your brain recognizes this as something which is happening. This visualization of successful accomplishments can contribute to your self-confidence.

When visualization is applied to the area of self-confidence, you are able to see yourself in your mind's eye accomplishing things on the baseball field which are under your control.

These accomplishments can include such things as attaining your goals, executing in a challenging game situation, performing effectively, and playing the game with confidence, among other things.

Here are some guidelines to follow when you want to use visualization in terms of your self-confidence:

1. Plan a time and select a place when you will spend time on visualization.

2. Be specific in what you visualize. Make it some process or aspect of your game that is clear in your mind and that is important to your self-confidence.

3. Only visualize things in which you are succeeding. Again, see yourself being successful at making progress at attaining your goals.

4. See yourself acting confidently.

5. Feel confidence in yourself in relation to that which you are visualizing.

EMPLOY AFFIRMATIONS THAT INFLUENCE YOUR SELF-CONFIDENCE

An affirmation is a statement that you make to yourself about yourself.

With respect to developing and maintaining your self-confidence as a baseball player, an affirmation is a statement which you make to yourself about some aspect of your performance on the field.

An example of an affirmation is: "I am able to locate my fastball inside". Another example is: "I stay back on the ball and inside of it".

When an affirmation is stated in the positive and when it centers on some specific part of your game, it is likely that you have contributed to the development of your self-confidence.

There are many ways that you employ affirmation in support of your self-confidence. Here are some guidelines for your use:

1. Make sure that the statement which you affirm has to do with a specific part of your game.

2. State the affirmation in a positive way.

3. Do not make the affirmation complicated; keep it basic and clear to you.

4. Use affirmations any time that you want to firm up your confidence. These times could be before the game in terms of your mental preparation and during it, between innings or even between pitches.

5. Make your use of affirmations part of your routine. Do not force using them. Make their use as natural as possible.

DEMONSTRATE CONFIDENT BODY LANGUAGE

Body language has to do with the way that you physically carry yourself during the game. It has to do with how you appear to others.

The language of your body particularly includes your torso and shoulders. To what extent do you look confident and composed or do you appear tentative and distraught.

For the most part, it is better for you to have command of your body and what it conveys to the opposition than to have poor body language. This kind of posture will bolster your confidence even if you do not feel confident.

Here are some guidelines to consider in terms of using your body language in support of self-confidence:

1. Become aware of the tendencies in your body language during the game. Identify the times and game situations when you tend to have good body language and those occasions when you do not.

2. Review your body language through video so that you can see how you look.

3. Maintain positive body language even when things are not going well for you.

4. Do not resort to body language which shows you as being overly emotional, tentative, or not assertive.

5. Get feedback from players and coaches about your body language.

ENGAGE IN PURPOSEFUL PRACTICE

You can do as much visualization and use as many affirmations as possible. However, unless you practice and have a purpose to your practice, you will not develop your game, and your self-confidence too will not develop.

Purposeful practice is a basic aspect of quality preparation and essential to self-confidence. It involves the following:

1. Be clear to yourself about what you are working on.

2. Make time for the practice or workout.

3. Engage in the drills and activities according to quality standards.

4. Monitor yourself on your effort and what you have accomplished.

MONITOR YOUR SELF-CONFIDENCE

During games, you can be aware of how confident you are in your beliefs that you are going to perform well. This is referred to as monitoring of self-confidence.

When you detect that your confidence is starting to drop off, then you can take the time to regroup and to bolster how you feel. In this respect, the use of visualization and positive affirmations are likely to be helpful during game competition.

During the course of the season, when you feel like you are losing your confidence, you can use the self-confidence checklist which appears as Table 9.1

TABLE 9.1. Baseball Self-Confidence Checklist

Baseball Self-Confidence Checklist

Review the areas below. For each area, rate yourself using this scale:

3: do this most of the time
2: do this sometimes
1: do this infrequently

Use this feedback to learn more about your self-confidence and then take steps to improve it.

1. I spend quality time in preparing, so that I am ready to compete.

2. I recognize when I start to lose my confidence and re-center myself on a confident feeling.

3. I use a key word, phrase, or image to keep me in a confident state.

4. I maintain positive and confident body language as I compete.

5. I keep my mind in the moment and on the correct pitch and do not let it drift.

6. I compare my execution and performance to myself and not to others.

7. I strive to compete against myself, day to day, so that I can be the best player possible.

EXERCISES

1. Think about a game situation or some point during the season when you were very confident and about which you were proud. How did you get yourself into this state? Describe the process you used.

2. Now, think about a game situation or some point during the season when you were not confident in your abilities. What were the reasons for this? What did you expect was going to happen? How was your body language?

3. To what extent are you able to detect your confidence? How do you make adjustments?

CHAPTER TEN

―――――― 🏐 ――――――

EMOTIONAL INTENSITY: GIVING CONSISTENT ENERGY AND EFFORT

The purpose of this chapter is to provide you with guidelines about how to effectively manage your emotions and their intensity as you play the game of baseball. Emotional intensity is the sixth mental domain of the Complete Mental Game.

Emotional intensity has to do with your emotions and how intense you are with them as you compete during the game, pitch to pitch, inning by inning, and also following the game.

As you compete, your emotions can be too intense, not intense enough, or just right in intensity for you. As a baseball player, your emotions will go up and down and, if left unchecked, your emotions can take you out of the game—they can hijack you.

Finding the best level of emotional intensity for a baseball player is an individual matter. There is no cookbook way to get at the right level. So, the information in this chapter will guide you in developing and refining your skills in productively managing the intensity of your emotions.

Emotional intensity reflects how you use your energy and how you display your effort. This occurs not only at the beginning of the game but throughout the entire period of time when you are in the lineup.

The use of your emotions and their intensity involves adjusting their level, up or down, so that your performance can be the best it can be for the game.

In order to increase your chances of performing well during the game, your intensity level needs to be just right for you. The energy and effort which you bring to the game must be coordinated with the demands and challenges of the game.

In this regard, your task is to not let outside factors such as the playing conditions of the field, the calls of umpires and fans, or other potential game distractions take your intensity out of a level where it is effective for you.

For the most part, there is a direct relationship between a baseball player's emotional intensity and how he performs. When a player's emotional intensity is too high, the player will tend to rush. More often than not, he will respond quickly, and becomes distracted, with a negative effect on performance being the result for him.

In contrast, when a player's level of emotional intensity is too low, the player typically is not engaged in the game. He becomes slow and lethargic, and his performance is not likely to contribute to the team.

However, when the player's emotional intensity level is just right for him—not too energetic and not too laid back—the player is emotionally into the game but does not overdo it. He takes the game one pitch to pitch at a time, and he is focused on the process of playing the game.

WHAT IT TAKES TO COMPETE WITH EFFECTIVE EMOTIONAL INTENSITY

To compete at just the right level of energy and effort during the course of a baseball game, you must rely on the purposeful use of your thoughts, emotions, and actions so that you can execute effectively throughout the game.

The good news in terms of emotional intensity is that all of these things—thoughts, emotions, and actions—are under your direct influence as a player. Consider, for example, the following position player who has been able to compete at an effective level of emotional intensity:

First, the player feels emotionally on an even keel during the game, whether he is in the dugout, in the batter's box, or on the field playing defense.

Second, he has developed a good emotional sense, just as if he had a built in thermostat. He knows what is too high and what is too low for him.

Third, the player is able to adjust his emotions, up or down, based on what he senses, by changing what he thinks about and what he says to himself.

Fourth, he makes sure that he stays in touch with his energy and effort and keeps at an effective level.

Finally, once the game is over, the player adjusts his emotions to a non-game, non-competitive level.

ADVANTAGES OF BEING JUST RIGHT WITH EMOTIONAL INTENSITY

There are many advantages to you, the baseball player, in being able to regulate your emotional intensity to compete and maintain it at just the right level for you. These advantages are the following:

1. You will get off to a solid start as the game begins.

2. You will feel confident and in control of how you are playing the game, since your emotions are working for and not against you.

3. You are likely to be more consistently focused on the task at hand, not letting emotions take you out of the game.

4. You will come across as being energetic as the game begins as well as during it

5. You will compete with a positive attitude. As a result, playing the game is likely to be more enjoyable than when emotions are not in control.

Think of baseball players you have seen or that you know and who bring energy and effort to the contest. How do these players look? How do they play the game?

DISADVANTAGES OF BEING TOO HIGH OR TOO LOW WITH EMOTIONAL INTENSITY

There are several distinct disadvantages to the player for not being able to remain at an effective level of emotional intensity. These are the following:

1. You may be limiting your self-confidence without a proper

level of emotional intensity, since your emotions are not aligned, in the moment, with the task at hand.

2. Your game performance may very well be below par, since your emotions will not working for you, by being either too high or too low.

3. You can experience increased tension and anxiety, due to negative emotions.

4. You are apt to be impatient without really knowing it, since negative emotions help to take the player's mind out of the moment and off the pitch.

5. Your physical fatigue and mental fatigue will probably increase as the game proceeds.

Think of players who seem to play the game with their emotions too high or too low. How do you think these players got themselves into these states? How do these players come across to you? What kind of impression do they make?

EMOTIONAL INTENSITY AND QUALITY OF PLAY

There are clear links between the level of a player's emotions, his intensity, and the quality of his play.

The manner in which a player uses his emotions and thoughts will very much affect how he responds during the game and the amount of energy he brings to playing it.

These relationships can be seen in Figure 10.1

Figure 10.1: Different types of emotional intensity.

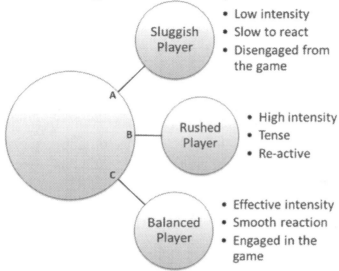

Figure 10.1 shows three players. These players are labeled as being as sluggish, rushed, or balanced in terms of their emotional intensity.

Perhaps you recognize yourself as being one or all of these players, at times.

The Sluggish Player—The emotional intensity of the player is lethargic and he is slow to react. It seems that he is bored with being on the field. Consequently, the quality of his play comes across as sluggish and his performance is below the standards set for him.

The Rushed Player—The emotional intensity of this player is rushed and he responds impulsively. The quality of his play is rushed and his performance does not typically mesh with what was expected.

The Balanced Player—The emotional intensity of this player is smooth and assertive. More often than not, the quality of his play meets expectations.

THE SLUGGISH PLAYER

If a player is *too low* in the intensity of his emotions during the game, then his play will be lethargic and slow. He will be a second or two behind things and his mind will not be in the moment, but very probably in the past.

The sluggish player may be thinking about things outside the game: what he did yesterday; what is going on at home; or other things.

The flow of the game passes the sluggish player by. His execution is likely to be less than expected. He may be referred to by coaches as not being in the game.

This player—the "Sluggish Player"—can be seen on Figure 10.1 as Player "A". When you look at this figure, you will see a player whose emotional intensity is low and whose play is sluggish and slow.

THE RUSHED PLAYER

If a player is *too high* in emotional intensity, then the quality of his play on the field will be too energetic and not smooth. His execution may reflect mental and physical mistakes.

This player is referred to as Player "B" in Figure 10.1 as the Rushed Player. He will be a second or more ahead of things and his mind will very likely be in the future. In this respect, he is likely to be thinking about results and about what others are thinking of his numbers. He overworks and overthrows. His energy and effort are misplaced.

THE BALANCED PLAYER

If a player is *just right* in terms of his emotional intensity, then his performance on the field will be energetic, coupled with good effort. This individual is referred to in Figure 10.1 as Player "C", the Balanced Player.

This player's mind will be in the moment, and on each pitch. He has been able to mentally park all else. He is able to compete throughout the contest.

GETTING EMOTIONAL INTENSITY JUST RIGHT FOR YOU

There are several steps which you can take in order to maintain your emotional intensity at a level which is just right for you.

Look these steps over and select the ones that can be helpful for you. These steps are:

1. Know your level of emotional intensity.

2. Conduct an emotional self-check.

3. Dial your emotions up or down, as necessary.

4. Maintain an even emotional feel.

5. Wind yourself down emotionally to non-game levels.

KNOW YOUR LEVEL OF EMOTIONAL INTENSITY

Before you can keep your emotional intensity at an effective level, you need to know what a good level is for you.

In order to learn more about yourself, go back and review games in which you have played very well. If you have video of these games, review your performance.

However, rather than focus on your performance in these games, get into the feel of how you played the game. What did it feel like? What were you thinking?

If you cannot access video, go back in your mind and think about these games and how you felt—how was your energy and emotion.

The intent here is to get the feel of your energy and emotion so that you can refer to that feel when you are competing. You can use it as a reference point to get back to an effective level.

CONDUCT AN EMOTIONAL SELF-CHECK

This involves getting a read on yourself as you get ready to play and as the game begins.

The time period at the beginning of the game can be important to how effectively you are going to compete. If you are sluggish, then you need to get yourself psyched up; if you are overly energetic, with too much energy, you will need to calm yourself down.

Here are questions which you can ask yourself before and during the game:

1. Are my emotions too high? Am I agitated or have too much energy flowing?

2. Are my emotions too low? Am I too sluggish and laid back?

3. Do I feel just right and ready to go?

4. Do I need to adjust my emotional intensity?

TURN YOUR EMOTIONS UP OR DOWN, AS NECESSARY

As the game proceeds, it may be necessary for you to regulate your emotions. Baseball is a game that involves your emotions and things can change during the course of a game which gets you out of a good emotional state and into one which you are either too sluggish or being too rushed.

Your ability to regulate your emotions—to turn them up or down at your command—is a key mental skill.

There are several things for you to consider and to be able to do, in this regard, and these follow below.

DIALING UP

First, in order to turn your emotions up (dial them up) you can energize yourself in the following ways:

1. Through physical activity—running or jogging in the tunnel or on the field.

2. By the use of visualization— seeing yourself performing at an effective and energetic level.

3. Using music as an aid.

4. Listening to tapes on which you have recorded statements that motivate and energize you.

DIALING DOWN

During the game you may find yourself starting to get too "emotionally high". This may be indicated by overthrowing if you are a pitcher, or by over striding on your swing in the batters box, or other things.

These are indicators which call for some emotional self-regulation—a lowering of your emotional level. Toward this end, here are some things to consider:

1. Step back and get into a deep breathing mode. This is one where you take a few deeps breaths from the abdomen area. This will have a quick calming effect on you and bring your emotional level down.

2. Get into the habit of shaking off your energy. Think of yourself as letting it go and feel yourself calming down.

3. Have some key words or phrases that have a calming effect. Words like relax, take it slow, slow down, are examples.

MAINTAIN AN EVEN FEEL

As the game begins and as it proceeds, you want to keep track of your intensity and not let it get too high or too low. Rather, you want to be able to remain on an even feel. This is a level where you feel energy in yourself and your effort is all there.

You can accomplish this very effectively for yourself. Periodically, during the game—between innings or at other times when there is a stop in the action, you can ask yourself the following questions:

1. Have I been assertive with my play?

2. Have I been giving quality effort?

3. Do I need to dial up or dial down?

WIND DOWN TO NON-GAME LEVELS

When the game is over, it is best to get into a state of emotion which is not baseball related. In this respect, the task is to "emotionally park" your game emotions and pick up those which define you in non-baseball settings.

In essence, this means, being able to focus on things that have to do with your life and core values and which have to do with other parts of your life. These may include things such as school or family.

You can pick up your baseball related emotional intensity, once you come back to the ballpark and prepare for the next game.

EXERCISES

1. Identify the times when you have had a tendency to become overly intense in terms of your competitive emotions. How have you handled these situations? Could you have done something to have regulated your emotional intensity to a more productive level?

2. Have there been times when you have become too laid back and even bored with the game? How did you handle these situations? Describe what you can do to prevent them from occurring in the future?

3. To what extent do you experience the emotions listed below when you play baseball? What usually happens that gets you into these states? What has been effective for you in getting out of the negative states and into positive ones?

    a. anger

    b. sorrow

    c. unhappiness

    d. not trusting teammates

    e. happiness

    f. satisfaction

    g. embarrassment

    h. not being locked in

    i. other negative emotional states

4. Interview a player whom you admire and whom you consider

plays the game with productive energy and effort. How can what this player says apply to you and your intensity?

5. Review a video of your performance in several games. What can you say about your emotional intensity? How would you describe it?

CHAPTER ELEVEN

———— ✐ ————

FOCUS: PAYING ATTENTION TO WHAT MATTERS IN THE MOMENT

Focus is the seventh mental domain of the Complete Mental Game. Focus is the area which has to do with your mind—and where it is—as you engage in the process of playing the game.

If you want to be successful in the game of baseball, it is important that you develop your capacity to focus.

Focus involves keeping your mind in the moment and on the task at hand as you play the game, and also knowing how to get back into focus when your mind drifts out of the moment.

Focus allows you to concentrate on what matters most and on what you can control, when it matters, and where you are at the moment. Focus involves all aspects of the game, from hitting to fielding, base running to pitching, to using your results to make adjustments.

In this respect, just how productive your focus will be as a baseball player will be determined by your understanding of what your primary task is at the moment and where your mind should be in relation to the task.

Focus involves knowing what the task at hand is and how to go about concentrating and locking into the moment.

Your capacity to focus on the process of playing the game includes three distinct time periods: before the game, during the game, and after the game.

Before the game, your focus is on preparing for the game, so that you are ready to compete when the game starts. Before the game, a basic task at hand for you is to implement a pregame routine, and to deal with other pregame activities, step by step. When you are taking batting practice, for example, your focus is on making solid contact and driving the ball. When you are involved in physical preparation, your focus is on things like stretching and running.

During the game, your focus is on being ready for each pitch and then how to react to the ball and the play. This is the case whether you are hitting, playing defense, pitching, or on the bases as a runner. In all of these instances, key questions are: Do I understand the game situation? Do I have a pitch that I want to hit, or deliver? Do I have a plan for accomplishing my task?

After the game, your focus is on reviewing your performance from the game. What were my pluses and minuses for the game? What did I learn from my performance? Do I need to make any adjustments? Then, once you have answered these kinds of questions, your focus after the game shifts to decompressing from the game and letting your game stay at the ballpark as you go home to focus on your family and friends.

Other Words that are used for Focus

There are words other than the word, focus, that are used by players and coaches to describe the state of being in the moment. Other words to describe focus include: attention, concentration, attention control, being locked in, or zoned in.

In the Complete Mental Game, the objective with respect to focus is to go beyond the specific words used. It is to understand what it means to be in the moment and to pay attention to what matters most, in the moment.

Locations for Your Mind

Basically, your mind can be focused productively only one of three places when you are playing baseball. Your mind is that part of you that involves the thoughts and emotions that influence your actions on and off the baseball diamond.

The three places where the mind can be focused at any one time are the following:

1. The *past*: This is the time when you think about things that have happened during the game, either when the game is over (how I performed), or as it is being played (how I gave

away my last at bat). It is best, for the most part, to allow your mind to be in the past, following the game, but not during it.

2. The *present:* This is the time when you are dealing with what is occurring in the moment as you play the game--- this pitch, this game situation, etc. When your mind is in the present, you are likely to be engaged in the game. When you are engaged in the game--- actively involved in it--- the more that your mind remains in the present moment, the better.

3. The *future:* This is the time when you are thinking about things which are going to happen but which have yet to occur and may never occur (what if I do not get out of the inning?; What if he throws me a slider and I cannot get to it?). Thinking about the future while you are competing is usually not productive.

In terms of the productive use of your mind and to maintain a consistent focus on what matters in the moment, it is best to center your attention on one of the above three time periods—but only at the right time.

There are times, though, when thinking about and focusing on the past is helpful (e.g., thinking about how you got the batter out the last time he was up). There are also times when it is important to think about the future (e.g., deciding what is my plan for my coming at bat).

For the most part, however, productive game performance in baseball occurs when your attention is given to the present moment, one step at a time, pitch by pitch. This kind of focus requires a quiet mind, which I will discuss later in this chapter.

When your mind is in the present moment, your full attention can be devoted to what is happening, there and then. However, when your mind is divided between two time periods—like thinking about the past and the present together—or if you are dealing with the past, present, and the future all at the same time, then the mind is too divided. You become distracted and your game performance is likely to suffer.

You are focused when your mind is centered in one time period, in the moment, and on one task at hand for that moment. When you are in the game and competing, the present moment is the best place for your mind to be.

ADVANTAGES OF BEING FOCUSED

There are several reasons why being focused on the right task and at the right time are advantageous to you as a baseball player:

1. You are more likely to remain alert and ready to react for the upcoming pitch and play, since you are paying attention to the task and, therefore, you are ready for it.

2. You can clearly hear what is being communicated to you by your coach as the game is being played, since you have no other influences trying to capture your attention.

3. You increase the likelihood of executing on the upcoming pitch, no matter what your role, since your full attention is centered on what is happening in the moment.

4. You feel more in control and in charge of the competitive situation, since the task has been reduced to the moment and extraneous factors have been minimized.

Think of players that you know or whom you have observed and whom you consider to be focused players. How do they play the game? How do you think that they got that way?

DISADVANTAGES OF NOT BEING FOCUSED

The disadvantages of not being focused as a baseball player include the following:

1. Lack of focus limits your personal engagement in the game, since your mind is in many places at the same time. You do not feel part of the game when you are not focused, since your attention is not squarely located on the game.

2. Limited focus increases the chances of physical and mental mistakes on your part, since your attention is not where it should be—in the moment.

3. Poor focus leads to distractibility, which can increase worry and tension.

4. When you are not focused, you are likely to be perceived by others, such as coaches and scouts, as not being engaged in the game.

Think of examples of players who have not been focused on some aspect of playing the game, like hitting, pitching or playing defense. What do you think are the reasons for the lack of focus of these players? How do you think that these players have become inconsistent in their focus?

THREE PLACES FOR YOUR MIND

In terms of your focus, the best place for your mind is on a specific time period and on the specific task that you want to accomplish.

In this regard, the tasks which you want to accomplish in baseball revolve around three distinct time periods: past, present, and future.

Although most of the remainder of this chapter deals with focusing in the present moment while you are competing, I will consider each of the three time periods.

FOCUSING ON THE PAST

Focusing on the past is very important to your baseball career and also to specific aspects of your overall development as a person.

Unless you review how you have performed and where you have been, you will be missing some important information.

However, there are only certain times when a focus on the past is productive.

Examples of situations when productively focusing on the past can be helpful to you are the following:

1. Reviewing your baseball career during the off season, using a step by step approach. This is a very good task for you to focus on during the off season as well as at other time periods when you are not playing the game.

2. Pinpointing the pluses and minuses of your game performance from the last game, but only once the game

is over. This is a very good task to focus on either directly following the game or on the next day.

3. Evaluating your last at bat. This can also be a good task to focus on, as long as it occurs well in advance of your next at bat and not while you are in the field or on the bases. The dugout is a good place for this, such as between innings.

FOCUSING ON THE PRESENT

When you are in the process of competing, the present moment is the place where your mind should be focused.

The present moment has to do with the now, what is occurring in the moment and on what you can observe and deal with without judging yourself.

Examples of focusing on the present moment are the following:

1. Committing to a pitch and delivering it to the catcher and his glove.

2. Seeing the ball and making solid contact with the ball.

3. Reading the movement of the pitcher to the plate when on base.

4. Throwing to the correct cutoff man.

FOCUSING ON THE FUTURE

When you want to consider where your career in baseball is headed, a focus on the future can be appropriate, but again only at the right time which is not during the game.

Although your baseball future has not yet occurred, you can plan for it, at the right time. Examples of focusing on the future are:

1. Deciding whether to play winter baseball.

2. Getting ready to plan for your retirement from the game.

3. Setting up a schedule with your strength and conditioning workouts for the coming week.

The Rhythm of Focus

There also is a rhythm to a baseball player's focus as he competes, between the lines. During the course of a game, a player's focus goes from a broad focus to a narrow focus and then back to broad and then back to narrow.

This rhythm of focus occurs, pitch by pitch. A player who is skilled at focusing has been able to get into a good rhythm with his focus.

The ability of the player to shift from broad focus to narrow focus constitutes the rhythm of focus.

Broad Focus

Before the hitter steps into the batter's box, or before a pitcher gets set to deliver the pitch, a broad focus is necessary.

This kind of focus allows the competitor to see the whole field in which he gets a sense of the game situation. The player is involved in a broad focus when he looks at the third base coach for the sign, decides what pitch to throw to the catcher, or plans where to hit the ball.

Whatever the inning or game situation, the focus of the player is broad and external and on things that are happening out there in front of him.

Narrow Focus

There comes a time during the game, especially between each pitch, when the player's focus needs to narrow, when it needs to center on the next pitch to be delivered. This is an example of a narrow focus.

For the batter, a narrow focus is seeing the ball and striving to make solid contact with it. For a pitcher, by looking at the catcher's glove and delivering a quality pitch to the glove, the individual manifests a narrow focus.

When a base runner who is on first base hones in on the first movement of the pitcher and proceeds to steal second base, this also is narrow focus.

The shifting of focus from broad to narrow and back requires that the player possess a quiet mind.

BEING IN THE MOMENT: THE QUIET MIND

The baseball player accomplishes the task of being in the moment and focusing on the task at hand by having a quiet mind. In this sense, the player with a quiet mind feels in control of himself. The game feels slow and not fast to him.

A quiet mind for a baseball player is a state of focus which has these characteristics:

1. The center of the player's attention is one pointed and calm. His mind is in the present moment, and not in the past or in the future. The player is honed in on the task at hand— seeing the ball, delivering a quality pitch, or reacting to the ball on defense, etc.

2. There is a positive feeling experienced by the player. The player is aware of what is going on around him. He observes what is happening in the moment, but there is no self-judgment in that the player is not thinking about himself or what others are thinking about him. The player feels good and he is ready to engage in the task at hand, without distracting thoughts. In essence, with a quiet mind, he is on automatic pilot.

3. There is no attention by the player with a quiet mind to his results or mechanics. The attention is on the process of playing the game and on the task at hand (hitting, fielding, pitching etc.)

4. The expectation for the player is that he will have an effect on the upcoming pitch. The player does not have doubt about his ability to execute. This breeds self-confidence on the part of the player.

BEING OUT OF THE MOMENT: THE DISTRACTED MIND

There are times during the game when the player's mind is *not* in the moment but it should be. In this respect, the player needs to understand and sense when his mind is distracted.

A distracted mind leads to a sense that the player is not in control of himself. He is not focused. Under these circumstances, the game starts to speed up on the player and mental and physical mistakes are likely to follow. A distracted mind is one that reflects the following:

1. The player's center of attention is scattered. It is not in the present moment. Rather, the player's mind is in the past with what has happened or in the future, worrying about "what if" something happens.

2. There is a feeling of distraction and doubt. The player sees what is happening but starts to make judgments about himself (Examples: My last at bat was poor; I am not doing well; What does the General Manager think about how I am playing?).

3. The player's attention is on results and possibly on other things like his mechanics or what coaches and others are thinking of him—when he is competing in the moment.

4. The player's expectation is to get results and not to pay attention to the process that is necessary in order to get the results.

GUIDELINES FOR DEVELOPING AND MAINTAINING YOUR FOCUS

As part of the Complete Mental Game, there are several ways that you can develop and maintain your focus so that you can increase your chances of keeping your mind in the moment, and quiet, as you compete. These ways are:

1. Use a mind in the moment process.

2. Implement an effective pre pitch routine.

3. Keep the mind quiet, with practice.

USE A MIND IN THE MOMENT PROCESS

There is a basic process that you can utilize that will get you in the habit of keeping your mind in the moment and focused on what matters, pitch to pitch.

It is not only a process but a mind set about how to stay focused on the process of playing the game. It reflects a way to play the game.

As part of the Complete Mental Game, this mind in the moment process goes by the name of MAC.

The concepts and procedures which form the basis of the MAC process were initially developed and researched by Dr. Frank Gardner and Dr. Zella Moore who are two sport and performance psychologists. Their work was based on some basic research in cognitive psychology and related psychological domains.

I have adapted this research and the MAC protocol of Drs. Gardner and Moore for use with baseball players and this approach has become part of the Complete Mental Game. The MAC process has three steps:

M: "Maintaining" mindful and meaningful contact with the present moment, no matter what the game situation or circumstance. In essence, you stay in the moment, no more, no less. Being in the moment involves *no floating* of your thoughts to the past or to the future.

A: "Accepting" what is happening in the present moment, no matter what the situation affords, whether favorable or unfavorable, by observing the situation but not thinking about yourself. Accepting what the situation affords involves *no judging* of yourself, or what you are doing or not doing.

C: "Committing" to the present moment and the task at hand, no matter what has to be done, without thinking of the situation or the outcomes. This kind of commitment involves *no doubting* of your ability to execute.

The steps of the MAC process are described, in more detail, as follows:

STEP 1: MAINTAIN CONTACT WITH THE PRESENT MOMENT
Mindfulness is being aware of the "baseball present". When you play the game, the present moment is all that you have. It is there for the taking… if you keep your mind in the moment.

Mindfulness involves just noticing what is there in the moment, but without judging or labeling it. Mindfulness involves staying in the moment and focusing on the task at hand, no more, no less.

Mindfulness is lost when your mind starts to float out of the present, drifting either into the past or into the future.

There are some things which you can use in order to develop your mindfulness. These are:

1. *Practice being an observer*—Just notice things as they occur, just as you would if you were sitting on a bank of a river and watching leaves float by. You can practice this before games or even at home. Just watch what is happening and what you are aware of. Try not to ask questions about these things; just be aware and observe. Work at maintaining contact with the present moment.

2. *Use deep breathing*—There is nothing more economical or helpful for being aware and staying in the moment than the use of your breathing. Deep breathing that is from the abdomen is something good to practice. When your mind starts to float or drift out of the moment, deep breathing can help bring it back into the present. Step back, take a deep breath, let it go and then focus on the task at hand.

3. *Shake off the tension*—When you are tense and restless, your awareness can easily be taken out of the present and you become distracted. Learning to relax can also help with your awareness and focus. I will address a method for progressive relation in the next chapter on composure.

STEP 2: ACCEPT WHAT IS HAPPENING

Acceptance is being willing to acknowledge and to feel the present experience, whether you like the experience or not. The experience of playing the game is basically the now, the present moment, and what is happening in it.

Accepting what is there in the moment occurs best when you do not bring along worry, doubt or speculation (the "what ifs") into it. Rather than fighting the experience or getting caught up in it, you simply observe what is there and accept it and then proceed to deal with the next pitch. You do not self-evaluate or judge at this time.

There are some things which you can do to help you with accepting what is there in the competitive moment. These are:

1. *Keep it impersonal*—Do not personalize the situation. Keep the facts of the situation (men on base; just committed an error) separate from your judgments about them. Using words like good or poor distract rather than focus your game.

2. *Embrace the now*—However, do not place yourself in it or attach yourself to what you are doing. Deal with the now but keep yourself out of the process. The game has too many ups and downs to ride the emotional roller coaster. The experience of playing the game is what it is all about, not by dragging yourself into it.

3. *Defuse your emotions*—Keep your emotions separate from the game experience. You do not want your emotions to hijack you and take you out of the game.

4. *Take "response-ability"*—You are in charge of your reactions to the situation. Do not avoid what you have to do in order to successfully execute on the next pitch. Your response may be an adjustment or stepping back, defusing your emotions from the situation, or other things.

STEP 3: COMMIT TO THE PITCH

The next pitch is all that you have; it is the only reality. The next pitch is your moment, the only moment. So, in order to get the most out of focus, you want to commit to the pitch.

Commitment to the pitch has to do with being ready, willing, and able to keep attention on the pitch or bring it back to the pitch if your focus starts to float.

In terms of competitive focus, everything comes down to the moment and commitment to the pitch.

Commitment to each pitch can be enhanced through the following activities:

1. *Being your best*—How you deal with each pitch reflects the kind of player that you are. If you are committed to your

development and being the best performer that you can be, then each pitch is a statement about your desire to do the best you can, in the moment.

2.   *Expect the effect*—The effect of your commitment to the pitch is what it means for the opponent. If you are a pitcher, for example, the delivery of the pitch means that you expect it to have an effect on the batter; it gets that batter one pitch closer to making an out. If you are a hitter, the next pitch can allow you to make solid contact and put the ball in play.

3.   *Look committed*—This has to do with your body language; what you look like and how you proceed with the pitch. So, whenever in doubt about being in the moment and committing to the pitch, display positive body language.

IMPLEMENT AN EFFECTIVE ROUTINE BETWEEN PITCHES

The time between pitches can very well be a make or break time for you as a baseball player in terms of your focus. This is the time when your mind can start to wander and you can become distracted and lose your focus.

This can happen whether you are a pitcher or a position player, and it includes both offense and defense.

In order to counter the tendency to lose your focus between pitches, it is helpful to have a routine that will enable you to maintain your focus.

An effective routine between pitches allows you to do the following:

• Let go mentally and emotionally of the last pitch.

• Relax briefly between pitches, without thinking and judging yourself.

• Get ready for the next pitch.

In this respect, here is an example of a routine for between pitches for a hitter:

1. Recognize what was the result from the last pitch (e.g., fouled it off, took the pitch, swung and missed).

2. Step back and out of the batter's box to give yourself a brief relaxation break.

3. Use some cue to relax yourself such as fixing your batting gloves or looking at the barrel of the bat.

4. Take a deep breath.

5. Step back into the batter's box.

6. Focus on seeing the next pitch and making solid contact with it.

7. Move on to the next pitch.

Here is a routine for a pitcher for remaining focused on the next pitch:

1. Observe the result of the last pitch, without judging it.

2. Get the ball back from the catcher.

3. Step off the pitching rubber for a brief relaxation break.

4. Use a visual cue (e.g., looking at the flag pole in center field) or a physical cue (e.g., rubbing the ball).

5. Take a deep breath.

6. Step back on the pitching rubber.

7. Expect to deliver a quality pitch.

During the course of the game, when you find yourself losing your focus, you can rely on your between pitch routine to get you back on track. This is the case whether you are a pitcher, hitter, or playing defense.

I will discuss regaining focus in more detail in the next chapter on composure.

KEEP THE MIND QUIET, WITH PRACTICE

You can learn to keep your mind quiet by learning and then practicing a very effective process called meditation.

Meditation is a process that can assist baseball players to achieve a more consistently focused and quiet mind.

Through learning and practicing meditation, you will become more skilled at staying in the moment and focusing on the task at hand. This will happen since your mind will become conditioned to being quiet and less likely to be perturbed.

Consequently, you will be in a better place, mentally and emotionally, to perform more effectively, since your mind will be in the moment, more consistently. You will not be distracted by concerns with failure or with expectations about success.

Through the disciplined practice of meditation, your mind can develop a constructive approach to dealing with various kinds of distracting situations that you are likely to encounter when you compete. These include distracting situations which are external to you such as umpires and field conditions, as well as those which are internal like worry about failure.

HOW TO USE MEDITATION FOR KEEPING THE MIND QUIET

When you use meditation as a process, your mind learns to recognize the potential distraction, acknowledge it, and then let it go by ignoring it, and not getting caught up in it.

During meditation practice, you focus your mind on one thing and one thing only. This one thing could be a number, your breath, a feeling, a key word, or another thing.

In order to use meditation, you need to be aware of the various forms. You should choose one. Here are three basic forms that you may be interested in:

- *Counting*: In this approach, you breathe in and out. Then, each time you exhale, you count one silently on the first breath, a two on the second exhalation, and a three on the third exhalation up to five. Then, you repeat again starting at one. Concentrate on counting and nothing else. When your mind wanders from the counting, bring it back into the moment and continue. Just observe where your mind is and do not judge when it wanders; just bring it back to the moment and onto the counting.

- *Breathing*: Follow the passage of your breath as it goes down into your diaphragm and back out again. Concentrate on the breathing and nothing else. When your mind wanders from the breathing, just acknowledge the distraction and bring yourself back to a focus on the breathing. Observe, breath, and do not judge

- *Key Word*: Select a word that has meaning for you like smooth, calm, solid contact, quick, etc. As you breathe in hear the word and as you breathe out say it. Then repeat. Concentrate only on the word. Say the word and do not judge.

Once you have selected a form of meditation which is comfortable for you, use the following guidelines for practicing the meditation process:

1. Know when you want to practice meditation

   a. You need to practice to become skilled at this process.

   b. You then can use it prior to each game and you can use it to quickly regain your focus during the game.

   c. You can use short bursts of meditation—5 to 10 seconds—to sharpen your focus during game competition.

2. Use a good posture

   a. Choose a quiet room or location either in the clubhouse or at home before you come to the ballpark.

b. Sit on a straight backed chair or stool. Keep your feet squarely on the floor. Place your hands flat with palms down on your thighs.

c. Do not stare at a spot on the wall or at a pattern. Rather, let your gaze be diffused.

3. Implement your method

a. This will be the counting, breathing, or key word approach described above.

4. Deal with distractions

a. You will be faced with distractions, without doubt (everyone does).

b. Simply acknowledge the distraction. Do not fight it. Rather, just let it go in your mind.

c. Gently bring your mind back to whatever you were concentrating on before you were distracted.

EXERCISES

1. Identify the times when you are most likely to lose your focus. Plan out steps which you can take to prevent or minimize your loss of focus from occurring.

2. Describe your pre pitch routine. Outline it and practice it, first using visualization and then physically in real time. Get feedback from others about your routine. Video tape yourself using it.

3. Advise another player on how to remain focused and to remain in the moment. Provide this advice for a player who needs help in the area and who would appreciate it coming from you.

CHAPTER TWELVE

―――――― ⚾ ――――――

COMPOSURE: REMAINING POISED UNDER PRESSURE

Composure is the eighth mental domain of the Complete Mental Game. Composure has to do with being able to remain in control of your thoughts, emotions, and actions as you compete, pitch by pitch, at bat to at bat, inning by inning.

Composure comes across on the field as being poised under pressure. When you are composed, you are not rattled by unexpected events. You do not lose it.

The extent to which you remain composed during a baseball game, and beyond, is seen in how you deal with the competitive stress, anxiety, and the perception of pressure.

Your composure comes to the fore and works for you when things are not going well, when your performance is less than expected, when you are facing adverse and unpleasant experiences.

In essence, when you are composed, you are able to manage your thoughts, emotions, and actions during the "thick" of competition.

When composure is lost, the baseball player allows negative emotions to "hijack" him. In essence, these negative emotions serve to take the player out of his game and away from the moment. This loss of composure then limits the player's effectiveness as a performer.

Opponents and coaches will typically describe a composed player, however, as someone who is poised and ready to get the job done, no matter what the score, or despite what just happened in the game.

THOUGHTS AND COMPOSURE

Thoughts affect how you, as a baseball player, manage the challenging and demanding game situations with which you are faced while you play the game. Thoughts influence your composure in the following ways

1. *How you think about the game situation*: Is the game situation considered as an exciting challenge for you to work through in a step by step manner? Or, is the game situation seen as a threat to self-esteem? Do you put pressure on yourself? Or, do you observe what is there and not judge it and just remain focused?

2. *What you say to yourself about the situation*: You believe that you possess the personal resources to remain in control of yourself (e.g., "I can rely on myself to stay cool, calm, and collected and get the job done"). Or, do you doubt your ability to cope and remain composed (e.g., "This is a big situation and the pressure is on").

3. *How you respond in the moment and in relation to the situation*: You can step back, regroup, and not lose control of your behaviors. Or, do you tend to worry and become unnerved?

EMOTIONS AND COMPOSURE

Emotions are the feelings that fuel your thoughts and actions, both on and off the baseball diamond.

According to a classification system which has been researched and developed by Dr. Richard Lazarus, there are two categories of emotions, both of which have relevance to baseball. These are:

1. Negative Emotions

2. Positive Emotions

NEGATIVE EMOTIONS

Some emotions can be considered as being negative and which occur because the player perceives harm, loss, or threat of some kind. For the most part, negative emotions tend to enable the player to lose composure with resulting decrements in performance. Examples of negative emotions are the following:

1. *Anxiety*: worrying about the next at bat or the next inning

2. *Anger*: being upset when you are taken out of the game

3. *Fear*: concern about failure and not making it to the next level

4. *Guilt*: feeling upset because you really did not prepare

5. *Sadness*: feeling down and out when you are left off the travel team

6. *Envy*: wanting what another player has

7. *Jealousy*: frustrated because you are not recognized by the manager like another player

POSITIVE EMOTIONS

The second category includes emotions which are usually considered as being positive and which result from benefits to the player. Examples of positive emotions are;

1. *Happiness*: being pleased with how you performed

2. *Appreciation*: embracing the coaching which you have received

3. *Pride*: feeling good about how you play the game

4. *Gratitude*: being thankful for the talent that you have been given

Stress, Pressure, and Playing Baseball

Competitive stress has to do with a player's perception about a game or about a particular game situation. Pressure is a label which players and coaches use to describe game situations. Pressure means "press", and when a player feels the press-ure, he feels expectations and the need to execute then begins to press down on him.

If a player considers the situation or the task at hand as a threat to himself, or if he believes that he is being put in some danger or risk that he cannot control, or if he feels pressed to get the job done, then he can very easily perceive the game situation as stressful . Consequently, he may label it as a pressure situation.

What we know from research about stress and its management is that these kinds of perceptions which a player makes about stress and pressure occur quickly and automatically and often below the level of consciousness.

In short, the player many times does not know that he is experiencing these negative emotions, until it is too late, when they take control and in essence hijack his focus and composure.

There are methods and procedures which a player can learn to apply that will help in the recognition of stress, anxiety, and perceptions of pressure and nip them in the "bud". Some very effective methods and procedures will be described later in this chapter.

Too much stress is harmful to the player's ability to remain composed—being in emotional command, with their mind in the moment.

Anxiety involves feelings of uneasiness that come about when a player is placed in situations which they consider detrimental or harmful and over which they believe which they have limited influence.

A mild form of anxiety is worrying about some task or about the results of one's performance. Stronger forms of anxiety include feelings of uneasiness, tension, and panic. An even stronger form of anxiety is fear.

Anger is an emotion which also is associated with loss of composure. In this sense, anger involves feelings about being frustrated—not getting what you want.

Often, anxiety which is associated with competitive stress includes not only an emotional component but also a physical component, which can lead to anger.

Stressful situations on the baseball diamond stimulate the anxiety of the player. In some instances, the player does not have the personal resources to recognize what is occurring and to make adjustments to get back into command of his emotions; then loss of composure is likely to occur.

Playing baseball involves coming in contact with many potential sources of stress and pressure. Any of these sources or a combination of them can contribute to loss of composure by a player.

Not too long ago, I conducted a confidential survey of baseball players at all levels of competitive play who were part of the Cleveland Indians Baseball Organizations.

As part of the survey, I asked the players to list things which have been stressful for them in baseball and which have resulted in them losing their composure. Table 12.1 lists examples of the responses of these players.

TABLE 12.1. List of people, places, and things that are stressful to professional baseball players.

1. Being recruited as part of the draft process
2. Deciding to sign a professional contract
3. Being away from home (homesickness)
4. Not having close friends around (loneliness)
5. Demoted to a lower level team (e.g., AAA to AA)
6. Promoted to a higher level team
7. Playing time (too little; too much)
8. Alcohol (use and abuse)
9. Tobacco (use and abuse)
10. Women
11. Relating to spouse/significant other
12. Illegal/non-prescription drugs
13. Nutritional supplements
14. Depression
15. Concentrating
16. Anxiety
17. Fear, worry, and doubt
18. Choking
19. Anger
20. Communication with teammates
21. Communication with staff
22. Dealing with the media
23. Developing friendships
24. Travel and hotels
25. Fans

26. Playing winter ball
27. Being taken off the 40 man roster
28. Being added to the 40 man roster
29. Physical Fatigue
30. Expectations
31. Being released
32. Physically injured
33. Surgery
34. Physical rehabilitation
35. Gambling
36. Bars/clubs
37. Finances
38. Continuing education
39. Pressures from family
40. Death of family/friends
41. Marriage
42. Divorce
43. Retirement
44. Playing every day (grind)
45. Taking directions
46. .....other

ADVANTAGES OF BEING COMPOSED

There are many advantages of being composed as the game begins and in remaining composed throughout the contest. These advantages include the following:

1. When you are composed, you have a feeling of being in control or command of yourself and how you play the game.

2. You have a sense of self confidence when you are composed, since you believe that you will remain in emotional control under competitive stress and pressure.

3. When composed, your mind stays in the moment and on the competitive task at hand, rather than worrying about things like what the coaches think of you or about what is going to happen to you next in the game.

4. In a composed state, you are able to take calculated risks

during the game, without the fear of being distracted or losing personal control.

Think of some baseball players who you know or who you have observed extensively and whom you consider to have good composure, as the game begins and as it proceeds.

What do these players do that leads you to the conclusion that they are composed or poised under competitive pressure?

DISADVANTAGES OF NOT REMAINING COMPOSED

Some of the prominent disadvantages to your performance when your composure is lost include the following:

1. You feel uneasy and tense as the next pitch or play begins to develop.

2. You are unable to concentrate and remain in the moment, due to worry and thinking about the past (what has happened already in the game) or about the future (what might happen later in the game).

3. Your emotions are inconsistent during the game, and you are caught riding the "emotional roller coaster": One inning you feel positive and next you find yourself in a negative state.

Identify some players who have lost their composure during baseball games or practices. What did these players do? How long were they in very emotional states? How do you think they got themselves into those emotional conditions?

A QUIET MIND AND A QUIET HEART: KEYS TO COMPOSURE

A quiet mind and a quite heart are two of the best leverage points which you can have to help you remain composed. This is the case whether you are a position player or pitcher, no matter what your role or your level of competition.

A quiet mind and heart will help you perform well on the baseball diamond and they will help keep you composed.

They can be very important when you are faced with game

conditions that can lead to competitive stress, and pressure, as well as at other challenging situations which you encounter as a baseball player, including stressful situations off the field.

When a baseball player competes, it is a natural tendency of the individual to press, to want to do well. This tendency, however, greatly increases the player's chances of losing composure; the player's mind becomes distracted and his heart starts to race; things speed up, spin, and become cluttered.

When the mind and heart are not quiet, the player starts to think about his needs and things that are out of his control, especially what others such as the manager and media are thinking about him. As a result, the player becomes very self-conscious while his physiology becomes less efficient; tension comes to the fore.

This mental and emotional process prevents the player from keeping his mind in the moment and his emotions under control.

Inevitably, both mind and heart speed up, spin, and race to the future, negatively affecting performance

A quiet mind and heart, though, set the stage so that you are more able to have things remain clear to you and you are more apt to be more focused and composed as you compete. You become and remain composed.

The states of having a quiet mind and a quiet heart are ones in which your thought process is clear and calm, while your heart rate is consistent and smooth.

With a quiet mind and heart, you are totally in the present. You are not thinking about the past or about the future. As a result, the game is moving slow and you see and feel it going that way. The game is not racing in your head or in your heart. Your breathing is deep and gentle.

You are ready for the next pitch, no more, no less.

A quiet mind, when coupled with a quiet heart, enables you to pay attention to the task at hand, without loss of emotional control, one pitch at a time. Your composure is there for you and for your performance.

HOW TO MAINTAIN YOUR COMPOSURE

In order to maintain your composure, you want to keep your mind and your heart quiet. So, how do you accomplish this?

There are several methods which you can learn to apply. However, learning and applying these methods does not come free.

All of these methods demand training and practice, before you can use the methods effectively. Here are some methods:

1. Mind in the Moment

2. Heart in the Center

3. Deep Breathing

4. Progressive Muscle Relaxation

5. Yoga

6. Biofeedback

Each method now will be discussed so that you can consider whether and to what extent, each one can be useful to you and your composure.

MIND IN THE MOMENT METHOD

There are times during the game when you are more likely to lose your composure than at other times.

Only you can best determine what those times are.

Here are some examples of game situations where the composure of baseball players can be at risk:

1. A pitcher quickly got two outs. Now, following several pitches, he has two men on base in scoring position.

2. A pitcher just gave up a three run, go ahead home run in the seventh inning.

3. A hitter strikes out for the third time in the game, with being caught looking on the third strike out.

4. A hitter gets hit in the back by a pitcher.

5. Fans are heckling and making derogatory comments to the left fielder.

The Mind in the Moment method is a practical and convenient way for quieting the racing mind, that is, a mind which is not quiet and which can be susceptible to loss of composure.

The Mind in the Moment method consists of three steps that are applied between pitches or at any other time during game competition when composure may be at risk. These steps are:

1. Red light the situation

2. Shift to neutral

3. Green light the next pitch

Here are the procedures which comprise each step:

Step 1: Red Light—"catch the racing mind and heart"

1. Identify the negative emotions that you are beginning to experience—frustration, anger, envy, revenge, worry, etc.

2. Pinpoint the negative sensations that go along with these emotions—shallow breathing, tension, restlessness, etc.

3. Accept what is present , without judging yourself

Step 2: Neutral—"slow things down by taking time out"

1. Mentally and emotionally shift to a neutral perspective, one where the mind and heart slow down.

2. Take some physical action like stepping off the mound or out of the batters box; or, if you are on defense, stepping back and disengaging for a moment between pitches.

3. Answer these three questions and use your responses to each question to adjust your mind and heart set:

    a. How is my breathing?—if shallow, make it deep with the use of deep breathing

b. Am I tense?—if tense, shake it off with some physical movement

c. Where's my mind?—if not in the present, bring it back to that spot by using a key word (e.g. "focus", or "present") or with some visual checkpoint (e.g., glove, sweet spot on the bat, flag pole)

Step 3: Green Light—"take on the next pitch with a quiet mind and quiet heart"

1. Step back mentally into the game situation.

2. Focus on the task at hand—the next pitch

3. Be relaxed and ready to execute

4. Commit to the task and follow through

5. Move on to the next pitch

HEART IN THE CENTER METHOD

The heart is an intelligent organ in and of itself. There has been considerable research about how the heart can help people to remain calm and composed.

The Heart Math Institute, which is based in California, has been a leader in the area of the heart and its intelligence by producing promising research and methods including computer software.

The Heart in the Center method is based on this research, and it is another way of helping you to maintain your composure during game competition.

This method, too, can help calm and quiet the mind and the heart. It differs from the Mind in the Moment method described above only that the focus is primarily on the heart.

Here are the steps of the Heart in the Center method:

1. Once you begin to experience emotions that can quickly allow you to lose your composure, step back mentally and

emotionally, off the mound; or out of the batter's box; or wherever you are on the field. Call a time out as needed.

2. Shift your personal attention from the field to the area around your heart in the center of your chest, just above your stomach.

3. Center your thoughts and feelings on your heart.

4. While doing this, feel something which is the opposite of the negative emotions which you are experiencing. Example are:

    a. Happiness

    b. Appreciation

    c. Calmness

5. Feel the positive emotion around your heart. Couple this positive feeling with deep breathing and see yourself in this positive state.

6. Step back into the competitive situation, with your mind and heart quiet.

DEEP BREATHING

The effective use of your breathing is a very economical method for maintaining and regaining your composure, if you know how to breathe deeply.

When you breathe deeply, you automatically begin to place yourself into a quiet state. Your mind becomes calm, while your heart rate becomes smooth.

You are able to pay attention to what is there in front of you in the game situation, rather than to what is inside of you, such as negative feelings.

However, many athletes, including baseball players, really do not know how to breathe deeply so that their breath can actually work for them and help with their composure.

Essentially, deep breathing is breathing from your diaphragm. Your diaphragm is a band of muscles that separates your chest from your abdomen. It is an area which is deep in your chest just above your abdomen.

Deep breathing involves inhaling and exhaling through your nostrils, not through your mouth.

Deep breathing is gentle breathing, not shallow or rushed breathing. It involves the filling and emptying of your lungs.

HOW TO LEARN DEEP BREATHING

In order to become good at deep breathing so that it can contribute to your performance and help maintain your composure, you need to practice this form of breathing. If you do not practice deep breathing, you will not become skilled at it where you can use it automatically during games. To practice deep breathing, use the following steps.

1. Imagine that you have a small feather on the tip of your nose, or you have some other object which could easily dislodge from the tip of your nose, like a drop of water or a coin.

2. As you inhale, breathe in deeply but gently, so that you do not dislodge the feather or object which is on the tip of your nose.

3. Then, exhale, which should be a bit longer than your inhalation. Here too, do this smoothly so that you do not dislodge the feather or object from your nose.

Practice this three step approach, over and over again. When you are learning this form of deep breathing, set aside about five minutes at a time, several times a day.

When you do this, think about game situations when you have tended to lose your composure. Imagine yourself breathing deeply and see yourself remaining in control of your emotions.

Remember, to breathe deeply, gently, and smoothly—never in a shallow way.

PROGRESSIVE MUSCLE RELAXATION

When you are tense, your performance is likely to suffer. This is so because your ability to be fluid and automatic in your movements is reduced.

This unnecessary muscle tension negatively affects the quality of your thoughts and emotions, which places you in an uneasy and agitated state.

When you are relaxed, you are more apt to be ready to compete, both as the game begins and throughout the contest, pitch to pitch. In this regard, you are more able to perform well.

The physical tension which you experience means that your muscle fibers are contracted. In contrast, when you are relaxed, your muscle fibers are in a relaxed state and more amenable to competition.

Relaxation is a natural process. By recognizing when your muscles are tense, you can quickly learn to relax them, progressively, step by step.

This competitive relaxed state will contribute to keeping your mind quiet, your heart working smoothly and efficiently, and your composure maintained. The likelihood is increased that your performance will be enhanced.

The following procedure is one that you can learn to become more skilled so that you can recognize muscular tension and relax your muscles in a progressive manner:

1. Sit in a straight backed chair; your breathing should be deep and natural.

2. You are now ready to progressively tense major muscles in your body. These muscles are grouped as follows:

   a. Right hand and arm

   b. Left hand and arm

   c. Both hands and arms

   d. Shoulders and neck

   e. Feet and legs

f.   Buttocks and abdomen

g.   Facial area

3.   Take each one of these muscle groups one at a time, beginning with the ones listed above. Now, tense each of these muscles for about ten second and inhale as you tense them. Then, relax each muscle group for about ten seconds and exhale as you relax.

4.   Repeat the sequence described in Step 3 above, about three to four times over each of the muscle groups for each practice session.

Once you become skilled at this four step procedure, it will become increasingly easier for you to relax on command during games.

This will happen because you will be more sensitive to detecting muscle tension and be quicker at relaxing your muscles because you will have practiced it.

THE PRACTICE OF YOGA

Yoga is a human art form and a disciplined practice that has existed for thousands of years. It helps people to remain centered, flexible and fit among other things.

Yoga has relevance for the Complete Mental Game, especially for the domains of focus and composure, and it also provides benefits for the physical side of the game.

Yoga encompasses training in stretching and flexibility. These areas are addressed through learning and practicing specific physical postures and poses, under the direction of a yoga instructor.

Through active involvement in yoga postures and poses, the individual learns to use their breath, and the process of breathing, to stay centered, and to keep their mind in the moment.

The practice of yoga is becoming increasingly used by baseball players. As part of the Cleveland Indians Baseball Organization, yoga has been used in worthwhile ways by pitchers and position players to enhance their performance by developing and refining their focus, composure, and flexibility.

As a baseball player, the practice of yoga has relevance to you and it is an area that I encourage you to learn more about. In this regard, yoga may very well have the following benefits for you, as a baseball player:

1. You can sharpen your perspective and personal awareness through learning how to cope with the yoga exercises and their challenges.

2. You will be provided an opportunity to develop your capacity to keep your mind in the moment.

3. You are likely to get better at using your breath as a calming mechanism which will help you maintain relaxed mental and physical states, on and off the baseball diamond.

There are various forms of yoga that cannot be explained adequately in the pages of this book. So, if you want to learn more about yoga and to find a qualified yoga instructor, speak with a psychologist or counselor who is knowledgeable about yoga.

In addition, perhaps you can locate someone who is involved with the practice of yoga either as an instructor or as a participant, and discuss with them the value of yoga to you as a baseball player.

BIOFEEDBACK: WHAT IT IS AND HOW TO LEARN MORE ABOUT IT

Biofeedback is another growing area that may be helpful to you in terms of learning to maintain your composure as that mental domain is described and discussed in this chapter.

Biofeedback is a method in which people are trained to improve their health by using signals from their own bodies. Whether you know it or not, you already have used biofeedback when you have checked out your weight on a scale or if you have taken your temperature. Both of these devices feed back information about aspects of your physical condition to you.

With respect to composure and baseball performance, biofeedback may have potential to be used to help players who are tense and anxious to learn to relax. However, this form of biofeedback must occur under the supervision of a health care professional who has expertise and training.

Biofeedback can help the individual learn to control certain body responses including the following:

• Brain activity

- Blood pressure

- Muscle tension

- Heart rate

- Skin temperature

There are various types of biofeedback including the following:
- Electromyogram (EMG)

- Temperature biofeedback

- Galvanic skin response

- Electroencephalogram(EEG)

If you are interested in learning more about biofeedback, consult with your team psychologist, physician or athletic trainer about how you can learn more about this method. The Biofeedback Certification Institute of America (BCIA) maintains a listing of qualified professionals.

EXERCISES

1. Identify the times and situations when you have lost your composure during game competition. Think about and describe each of these situations. What would you have done differently now if the situation were to present itself to you?

2. Identify a particular pressure packed game situation in which you maintained your composure. What did you do that allowed you to remain composed? How can you build what you did into your competitive process?

CHAPTER THIRTEEN

---------- ◯ ----------

TEAMWORK: RELATING PRODUCTIVELY TO TEAMMATES, COACHES, AND OTHERS

Teamwork is the ninth mental domain of the Complete Mental Game. In this regard, teamwork is an area of baseball that involves each and every player, no matter what is the role of the player. Teamwork includes how the individuals on the team relate to one another, and how they work together, so that the team can be successful.

For team members to work together effectively and for the team to be successful there needs to be a chemistry or harmony. In other words, there needs to be a balance between the individuals who are on the team and their needs and how they interact as a collective entity in terms of team goals.

Teamwork begins with the individual who is on the team and his desire to embrace the team, to be a good team member, which means to be a positive contributor to the team.

In this chapter, the focus is on the development of the individual baseball player as a good team member and not on the team development.

The center of attention in this chapter will be on the baseball player and how he relates to and works with teammates, coaches, and others.

TEAMWORK AND THE INDIVIDUAL PLAYER

At the level of the individual player, teamwork has to do with how the player relates to the people with whom he comes in contact as a baseball player. This includes how the player communicates with others, both teammates and coaches alike as well as how, and when, he might take on the role of a leader.

These interactions occur throughout game competition as well as off the field, before the game, and following it.

There are a range of individuals and groups whom the player needs to relate and communicate with during the game, and at other times.

Here is a list of people, along with some examples of how the player can be a good teammate through productive interactions:

1. *Coaches and instructors*: The player needs to listen to and respect coaches and instructors during game, including doing things like getting signs from them and seeking advice from them.

2. *Teammates:* The player needs to be on the same wave length with teammates with respect to how to execute during the game, doing things like following through on cutoffs and relays, hitting behind the runner; or being a team leader.

3. *Opponents*: The player needs to respect the players on the other team as people and fellow baseball players but then be prepared to go out and compete against them as performers.

4. *Athletic trainers*: The player needs to allow trainers and related support staff to offer advice and assistance to them before, during, and following the game.

5. *Baseball administrators*: The player needs to understand the intentions and expectations of general managers, athletic directors, and others about the player and his status and place in the organization.

6. *Umpires:* The player needs to acknowledge calls and decisions made by umpires, while respecting the job that they have.

7. *Fans*: The player needs to be positive and open, without getting too close or personal with fans.

8. *Media:* The player needs to understand the role of the media and provide them appropriate time and responses.

9. Others

Teamwork has to do with the quality and appropriateness of the relationships which you have with the above individuals and groups.

Without good teamwork, both the player and the team are at distinct disadvantages. In essence, teamwork involves interacting productively with others who are associated with the team.

Leadership, which is the ability of the player to guide and influence team members, is a part of effective teamwork. I will cover this area of leadership later on in the chapter.

ADVANTAGES OF BEING A GOOD TEAM MEMBER

There are distinct advantages to being a good team member. When you are a good team member, you add value to yourself as a baseball player since you will be contributing to the success of the team.

When you are a good team member, the following benefits are likely to come your way:

1. Scouts and others who are evaluating your baseball skills and abilities will be quick to recognize that you are willing to do your share on and off the field.

2. You will be understood by your teammates and coaches as an individual who is willing to be part of something that is larger than their own self.

3. You will be able to have more productive and satisfying contact with coaches and teammates, since you are not thinking only of what is in it for you.

4. You will lessen the likelihood that you will be misunderstood by your teammates.

5. You will be more effective at your execution since teammates will know what you need to do and what you have to do.

6. When the time is right, you can leverage your potential to be a team leader.

Think of players that you know or who you have observed that you consider being effective teammates. Why are they this way? How have they helped the team?

DISADVANTAGES OF NOT BEING A GOOD TEAM MEMBER

By not being a good team member, however, the player places himself at a disadvantage in many ways. These ways include:

1. Scouts and others who are evaluating your baseball skills and abilities will pick up on your reluctance to be a good teammate rather quickly and they may very well perceive you as being self-centered and not a team oriented player.

2. Difficulties are likely to occur for you in relating positively to coaches and with teammates.

3. You may be misunderstood as to your intentions and motives.

4. You will be less likely to understand the intentions and motives of teammates and coaches.

5. Your execution may be diminished since communication with teammates may not be occurring as necessary.

INDICATORS OF BEING A GOOD TEAM MEMBER

There are various indicators that will enable you to know if you are a good teammate.

In terms of the Complete Mental Game, a good team member is being defined as follows:

A baseball player who relates productively and respectfully to teammates and coaches, and who consistently does his job on and off the field.

Based on this definition, there are eight indicators which signify that a baseball player is being a good team member. These indicators are the following:

1. Respecting the Game

2. Staying Balanced

3. Knowing Your Role on the Team

4. Communicating with Coaches and Teammates

5. Resolving Differences of Opinion

6. Interacting with Umpires, Media and Fans

7. Being a Team Leader

8. Monitoring Your Contributions to the Team

RESPECTING THE GAME

The game of baseball is bigger than any one individual. There is a right way and a wrong way to play the game.

You are being a help to the team, and not a hindrance to it, if you recognize your place in the larger perspective of the game. This is the case, no matter how much talent you have or how above average your performances may have been.

There is no better way to be a good teammate than to respect the game of baseball and how it is supposed to be played.

Respecting of the game can be seen in the following actions which you can take as a teammate:

1. Being on time for all practice sessions and team functions.

2. Giving consistent and quality effort at all workout, batting practice, and bullpen sessions.

3. Running out all ground balls during games.

4. Being attentive and engaged in the game, even if you are not in the lineup.

5. Not showing up teammates, coaches, or staff.

6. Congratulating teammates who have scored and who have been productive such as hitting a home run.

7. Not interacting with fans while the game is being played.

8. Other related actions.

To respect the game means that you care for the game and that you care about your team. In this regard, you are being a good team member.

STAYING BALANCED

Playing the game of baseball is hard, no matter what level of competitive play you are at. In this respect, players who are trying to get to higher levels often find it challenging to stay balanced: They want to help the team and contribute to winning, but they also want to do well themselves, be noticed, and get to advance to a higher level of competition .

In essence, every baseball player has to come to grips with the WIIFM/WIIFT balance, which is a very important area for being a good teammate.

WIIFM is an acronym. It stands for the following question:

What's In It For Me?

In order to be a good teammate, you should be clear with yourself about how you are going to answer that question.

Toward this end, the best answer for you is to focus on your development, to strive to be the best that you can be today and every day, on and off the field.

In this way, you can monitor yourself against yourself and be ready to contribute when you are called upon to do so. In so doing, you are being a good teammate.

WIIFT also is an acronym. It represents the following question:

What's In It for the Team?

Here, the best response to that question is to be ready to contribute through being the best that you can be on that day. In this way, you are contributing to the team.

By being the best that you can be, you are contributing to the team by being ready to compete and to do your best at the time you are called upon. You are being a good team member.

KNOWING YOUR ROLE ON THE TEAM

Being able to know what your role is on the team is not an easy matter. However, knowing your role on the team is a very important indicator of being a good teammate.

In order to know your role on the team, you need to get specific and be specific with your manager or coach.

Your role on the team really reflects what you are expected to do, how you can contribute to the team, and why this role is important to the team.

In order to clarify and know your role on the team, make it a point to discuss the following three questions with your manager or coach:

What is my role on the team?

1. How would you like me to fulfill this role?

2. What do I need to do in order to get better at this role?

Examples of roles that baseball players are expected to fulfill as part of being a good teammate are the following:

- Getting on base, in the role of being leadoff hitter in the lineup

- Putting the ball in play with men on base

- Giving the team a chance to win the game in the role of a starting pitcher

- Getting left handed hitters out in the role of a left handed relief pitcher

- Playing quality defense

- Being a team leader on and off the field in the role of being a veteran player

Communicating with Teammates and Coaches

Communication has to do with your ability to get your message across to someone else on the baseball diamond as well as to understand the message of another individual. The people with whom you want to communicate with most regularly are your teammates and coaches.

There are many opportunities during a game when it is important for you to communicate your message as a good team member. Some examples are the following:

- Letting the fielder know to which base the ball is to be thrown on a bunt play

- Telling the infielders where to position themselves

- Receiving the sign for the hit and run play from the third base coach

- Reassuring a pitcher to calm down following his giving up a home run

- Discussing how to make adjustments to the lineup with the pitching coach

Communication also involves being able to determine how your message was received by a teammate or by a coach.

In this sense, communication is a two way street and one that requires attention and listening on your part.

In communicating with teammates and coaches, here are some guidelines:

1. Strive to get your message across to the other individual in specific terms—What point do I want to make? How will I make it? When? Why?

2. When communicating a point, focus on concrete behaviors and facts, not on generalities and vague opinions.

3. Ask for clarification when things are not clear to you.

RESOLVING DIFFERENCES OF OPINION

The ability to resolve differences of opinion with teammates and coaches is part and parcel of being a good team member.

Nothing in the game goes smoothly all of the time. Examples of things being at odds with a teammate or coach are the following:

- Not agreeing with your catcher on the pitches necessary to get a hitter out

- Seeing your performance from the last game as different than the opinion of your manager

- Considering whether you should tell the manager or coach that you are not feeling good and to keep you out of the lineup

- Believing that you warrant more at bats than you have been getting

- Feeling that you have not been used appropriately in the game, being removed for a pinch hitter

Without a doubt, differences of opinion like the ones listed above will come to the fore as the game and season proceeds, and conflict surrounding these differences needs to be managed.

It is better to deal with these differences of opinion about playing baseball early on rather than later. Being able to nip things in the bud is being a good teammate. Here are some guidelines in this area:

1. Be respectful of the role and authority of the other person.

2. Ask for clarification about the situation at which you are at odds.

3. Do not deal with generalities or with personalities.

4. Be specific and factual with your concern.

5. Remain composed and under control of your emotions.

6. Consider the situation as a challenge but as one which can be resolved.

7. Engage in mental practice of how you are going to handle the situation before you go through with it.

Interacting with Umpires, Media, and Fans

The phrase "being a loose cannon", readily applies to this indicator of being a good teammate. In the baseball culture, a 'loose cannon' often is used to describe a player whose behavior is unpredictable and which could have a negative effect on the team. Examples of "loose cannon behavior" include the following:

- Disrespecting an umpire by intentionally trying to show the umpire up during the game.

- Making negative statements about an umpire or an umpiring crew to the media.

- Refusing to talk with the media by not showing up to a previously arranged meeting

- Making derogatory gestures to fans.

Being a good teammate means not disrespecting umpires, media, and fans. Rather, it requires that you interact appropriately with roles that these groups play. This kind of commitment requires personal awareness, mental discipline and composure on your part.

First, in terms of personal awareness, you need to keep in mind the roles that umpires fulfill in terms of baseball and to use these roles as your anchor points in dealing with these constituencies:

Umpires: They are responsible for calling an objective game in terms of balls and strikes and other areas of the game, and do this under a range of conditions.

Media: They are expected to report on the game and the

situations which surround the game and to do so in an objective and fair manner.

Fans: They are present at the ballpark to enjoy the game, and while there, not be disrespectful to players.

Second, in terms of mental discipline, you can benefit from knowing when and how you are going to interact with these three constituencies:

Umpires: There are times during a game such as during time outs or when the side has been retired, when you can approach umpires and ask them questions. This can occur in a quiet one on one manner and not in a disrespectful way.

Media: The best place to deal with the media is in the clubhouse before the game or at a time which you set aside to speak with them. Once the game is over, which can be an emotional time, plan out when you will address them, such as following your shower, after getting something to eat, etc.

Fans: Have a plan for when you will speak with them---before the game is typically the best time.

Third, with respect to maintaining your composure, consider the following:

Umpires: Never seek to show up an umpire. It is better to walk away and not say anything rather than let out emotions on the umpire.

Media: Be cautious about your comments and commitments. It is better to not comment or to be factual if you are not sure than say things which you may later regret.

Fans: Do not acknowledge or interact with fans when you may lose your composure.

Being a Team Leader

It is not easy to be a team leader. In addition, not everyone can and should assume a leadership role on the team.

Being a good team member means knowing whether and to what extent you should take a lead with the team.

Every player is not cut out to be a team leader.

In addition, there are various types of team leaders; some are quiet and reserved and let their play primarily do the leading. In contrast, other players are more outgoing as leaders of their teams.

With respect to being a team leader, here are some things to consider for being productive in that teamwork role:

1. *Have you established yourself on the field of play?* If you have not demonstrated that you can perform on the field, it may be best that you reserve your role as a leader. If your performance has been consistently good, you may be in a better place to take on a leadership role.

2. *What is your message?* As a team leader, you want to let teammates know where you stand not only through words but actions. This is your "message" as a team leader. It should be clear and it should let your teammates know what you stand for as a team leader. Your message may reflect any of the following kinds of intentions which are examples only: Being the best team possible; playing the game the right way; getting after it one day at a time; other.

3. *How is the quality of your preparation?* If you are going to be a leader, it is important for other players to see that you take your preparation seriously.

4. *What do teammates think of you?* Teammates will have certain perceptions of you. You need to take these viewpoints into consideration when taking on a leadership role. In this sense, there may be teammates that you need to talk with about how you plan to proceed so they know what is happening. These perceptions are important for you want the teammates to rally round your cause to make the team the best team possible.

5. *How balanced are you?* As a team leader, you want to continue to develop yourself and your overall game. In addition, you want to buy into the team to have it be the best that it can be, with your leadership.

6. *Are you willing to step up?* Being a team leader requires that you make your voice heard and your opinion known during the game, especially when things are not going well as well as when players may be dogging it. Being a team leader in this respect requires that you let teammates know if they are playing the game the right way.

7. *Do you help others?* A team leader is willing to lend a hand with helping other players to be the best which they can be.

8. *Can you accept the good with the not so good?* As a team leader, you need to be there for the team and with the team when it is winning and at other times.

9. *How will you relate to your manager or coach?* Every team leader has a way of letting the manager or coach know what it going on and serving as a coach of sorts on and off the field.

10. *Will you put in the time?* Being a team leader takes time, so you need to be willing to accept this responsibility and the time needed to be a team leader.

MONITORING YOUR CONTRIBUTIONS TO THE TEAM

If you are going to be a good team member, you should be willing to monitor yourself on this area.

Toward that end, you can check yourself out every so often about how you have contributed to the team as a team member.

Here are some things which you can evaluate yourself on:

1. Have I been respecting the game?

2. Am I maintaining a good balance between my development and that of the team?

3. Do I know my role on the team and how have I been in accepting it?

4. How has my communication been with teammates and coaches?

5. When differences have come up, did I resolve them effectively and with respect for others?

6. How have my interactions been with umpires, the media and fans?

7. Has it been my place to be a team leader and have I been willing to assume that role?

EXERCISES

1. When have you been productive in communicating with teammates and coaches? How have you done this? How have you felt during these times?

2. When are times when it has been difficult for you to communicate? To whom? What have you typically done? What have been the results?

3. To what extent do you consider yourself to be a team leader? Why or why not?

PART FOUR

ACCURATE SELF-EVALUATION: BEING REAL ABOUT RESULTS

CHAPTER FOURTEEN

———— ⚾ ————

SELF-ESTEEM: BEING A GOOD SEPARATOR

Self-esteem is the tenth mental domain of the Complete Mental Game. It involves being a good separator. In this sense, a good separator is a baseball player who does not allow the performance side of his life, what he does on the baseball diamond, to limit or negatively affect the personal side of his life, what he does off the field.

Being a good separator is the basis for developing and maintaining positive self-esteem in baseball. When you can keep your performance separate from yourself as a person, you can remain on an even personal keel, more often than not, on and off the baseball diamond. Your self-esteem will develop in a positive direction.

Self-esteem—what you think about yourself over and above baseball—is a mental domain which is crucial to the competitiveness and performance of all players, no matter what their level of competitive play.

Whether you are at high school, college, or the professional level, your self-esteem can make or break you.

Positive self-esteem—being able to separate out the performance side from the personal side—increases your capacity to focus on the process of playing the game, without anxiety or distractions.

Unfortunately, self-esteem often is misunderstood by some baseball players and some coaches as to what the area encompasses and how it can affect game performance and life in general.

Some of these individuals prefer to make light of self-esteem or otherwise consider it a sign of weakness if the player needs to address their self-esteem.

Self-esteem has to do with you and your "self", especially what you think about yourself and the extent to which you respect or esteem yourself.

Positive self-esteem is the state where the baseball player regards himself as a person positively and with humility, no matter whether his performance and results are good or not so good.

SELF-ESTEEM CHALLENGES

In developing and refining your self-esteem so that it can be positive and work for you, there are two basic challenges that you as a baseball player need to address.

One basic challenge has to do with the continuous development of your self-esteem. The challenge involves becoming skilled enough so that you do not get down about yourself, when things are not going well at bat, in the field, on the mound, etc.

In other words, you are able to separate out your poor game performances for what they are—performances that did not occur as planned—from yourself as a person who has a life to live, over and above the game.

This kind of mind set is important because baseball is a game of failure. In the day to day environment of playing baseball, it is easy for the player to get down, out, and discouraged about himself and to take things personally.

Beating yourself up mentally and emotionally is not a fair way to treat yourself in the game of baseball. Playing baseball at any level of competition is hard work, although it can be enjoyable process at the same time. As a result, it is easy to fall into the trap of letting performance leak into your personal side and negatively affect it.

When you are not doing well, it is easy to get down on yourself—to beat yourself up so to speak. Self-esteem, or lack of it, can affect performance, for better or worse.

The second basic challenge for the continuous development of your self-esteem as a baseball player is to be able to make sure that you do not "get up about yourself". In other, words, you do not allow yourself to think so much of yourself that you get a "big head" and become cocky.

This is especially important when your performance is at or even above what is expected. In these situations, you need to remain humble and grounded, and positive self-esteem helps in this regard.

A baseball player with positive self-esteem is someone, therefore, who stays on an even personal keel. In order for positive self-esteem to occur, however, the player needs to be a good separator.

This means that the player can separate out his performance from his "self" as a person, within and over and above the game.

This kind of player—the one who is a good separator—is able to keep himself as a person out of his performance. Consequently, he is able to remain on an even personal keel about his performance, his overall game, and his life.

Self-esteem also is very closely aligned with two other of the mental domains of the Complete Mental Game. One of these domains is perspective which has to do with being able to balance baseball and life. The second mental domain is personal awareness, which has to do with knowing yourself.

TWO PARTS OF SELF-ESTEEM
Self-esteem is made up of two parts. These are;

Self + Esteem

The "Self" part of self-esteem has to do with who you consider yourself to be, as a person. In this sense, your self is made up of your values, preferences, attachments and the images which you have of yourself.

The "Esteem" part of self-esteem has to do with personal evaluation— the kind of personal regard which you hold for yourself. Esteem has to do with the judgments that you make about yourself and the value you believe that you have as a person.

Baseball, of course, is one thing you value and with which you identify. Over identification with baseball to the exclusion of the rest of your life will be distracting and confusing. If you define yourself as a person by baseball to the neglect of yourself as a person, you are likely to be disappointed, since baseball is a game of failure.

WHAT SPECIFICALLY NEEDS TO BE KEPT SEPARATE?
If you want to maintain positive self-esteem as a baseball player, then just what needs to be separated?

In essence, there are four levels of your psychological development which require separation. These four levels have been presented and discussed in detail in earlier chapters of the Complete Mental Game.

The four levels of your psychological development as baseball players are summarized here as follows:

I.   The Player as a Person: Your personality, core life values, vision for success.

II. The Player as a "Coper": Your skills for coping with people, places, and things.

III. The Player as a Teammate: Your willingness to be part of something beyond yourself.

IV. The Player as a Performer: Your preparation, competitiveness, and evaluation of your performance.

Levels I and II, which deal with the personal side of the player, need to be acknowledged and be separated out from Levels III and IV.

You can be a good person, independent of baseball.

In a similar way, Levels III and IV, which deal directly more with performance, need to be kept separate from the other two levels.

During the course of the season, you can perform well, or not so well, but your performances and your judgments about how you perform should not leak or run over into one another.

Figure 14.1 is a visual illustration of these four levels, as aligned with self-esteem and how they need to be separated.

Self-Esteem

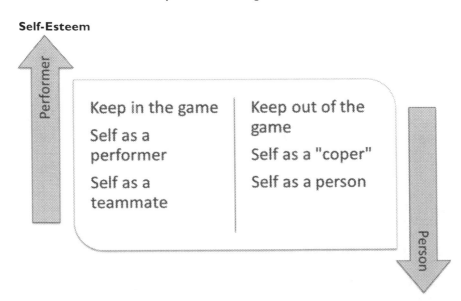

The first area for separation is that of the *Player as a Person*. This includes the player's values, personality, family and friends. This level defines the player as a basic human being. This level is present whether or not the individual is a baseball player.

The second area for separation represents the *Player as a "Coper"* including how he adjusts to the ups and downs of daily life. This area too exists independent of whether or not the individual is a baseball player.

The player as a person and a "coper" is best reserved for family and friends and is best mentally parked at the clubhouse room door. You can pick them up again, once the game is over.

The third level for separation is the *Player as a Teammate* while the fourth level for separation is the *Player as a Performer*, as seen in Figure 14.1.

The third and fourth levels have to do with the game of baseball and being in the moment, dealing with that which is there in front of you, pitch by pitch, at bat by at bat, as the game proceeds.

These third and fourth levels involve playing the game of baseball— how you prepare, the energy and effort which you bring to the game and display as the game proceeds, and how you evaluate your performance.

These levels too are best mentally parked as you leave the clubhouse. They are not you as a person.

ADVANTAGES OF POSITIVE SELF-ESTEEM

Positive self-esteem can be considered as being the state in which the baseball player regards himself positively but humbly as a person, no matter what his results are, at any given time, on the baseball diamond.

In terms of positive self-esteem, if the performance of the player is poor and if he has positive self-esteem, he will not beat himself up about this poor performance. Rather, he will take concrete actions to improve his performance but he will keep his self as a person out of the process. He will keep person and performance separate.

In contrast, if his performance is good, the player with positive self-esteem does not get a big head but continues to stay within his plan. With positive self-esteem, the player enjoys life, including playing the game as well as being over and above it. This player is a good separator.

There are many advantages for you in possessing positive self-esteem as a baseball player. These advantages include the following:

1. You feel very good and enthusiastic about yourself.

2. You enjoy the process of playing the game.

3. You are willing and receptive to take calculated risks and to follow through with decisions on the baseball diamond.

4. You tend to be appreciative of life.

5. You cope effectively with obstacles to baseball success and to the quality of life.

Think of players whom you believe exhibit positive self-esteem. What is it about these players which lead you to this conclusion?

How do these players deal with the day to day of playing baseball? What about their lives off the baseball diamond?

DISADVANTAGES OF NOT HAVING POSITIVE SELF-ESTEEM

Not possessing positive self-esteem can be referred to as having negative self-esteem.

In this regard, negative self-esteem reflects a baseball player who has difficulties with the separation of performance from the person. This individual identifies with his performance and attaches himself to it.

When his performance is not good, the player takes it personally. He devalues himself.

In addition, when performance is good or better than expected, he over values it and identifies with it.

In both cases, the player's identify is based on the game. His life is not balanced with the game. He does not remain on an even keel.

Disadvantages of not having positive self-esteem include the following:

1. You can feel down and out about your future.

2. You may tend to be unhappy and pessimistic about your game and life.

3. You are tentative at taking competitive risks or making decisions, due to the possibility of failure.

4. You can drift into dissatisfaction with playing the game and possibly with aspects of life.

Think of players who you think possess negative or poor self-esteem. How do they deal with their performance and with people, inside and outside of the game?

GUIDELINES FOR SELF-ESTEEM

In the remainder of this chapter, I will provide a range of guidelines that can help you manage your self-esteem as a baseball player and as a person. The following areas will be covered:

1. Mentally Park the Person

2. Put on the Role of the Performer

3. Be Mindful of the Moment

4. Keep Self Judgment out of Your Performance

5. Use Positive Self-Talk

6. Visualize Positive Actions

7. Look for the Small Wins

8. Take a Personal Inventory

9. Watch Out for the Big and Little Head

10. Enjoy the Process

MENTALLY PARK THE PERSON

One way to help foster positive self-esteem throughout your baseball career is being able to "mentally park" yourself as a person.

Mental parking means being willing and able to leave the larger scheme of your life—yourself as a person—at the door of the clubhouse. By doing this, you can focus on your baseball life inside the clubhouse and on the field.

In essence, through mental parking, you leave yourself as a person out of the process of playing the game and you start to focus on yourself as a performer.

The game of baseball is hard enough. You do not need your personal cares and concerns to seep in and affect your self-esteem and influence how you prepare and how you compete.

By mentally parking yourself as a person at the clubhouse door, you are likely to receive the following benefits:

First, you limit the process of playing baseball from being intertwined with the process of the rest of your life. This is important since your life includes values, cares, and concerns, over and above the game, all of which relate to your self-esteem.

Second, through mental parking, you can focus your efforts on the process of your preparation and the process of competing, without your life entering into the picture.

Third, when you evaluate your game performance, yourself as a person will not be part of this self-evaluation. You will be better able to keep yourself out of it and focus more clearly on the specifics of your performance—what you did well and what you did not do well.

Here are suggestions to consider for the mental parking of yourself as a person at the clubhouse door:

1. Before you enter the clubhouse, make it is point to "hang up" your thoughts and concerns as a person on an imaginary hook. Or, place your thoughts and concerns as a person in an imaginary safe, just as you would for your wallet, wrist watch, ring, and other items.

2. When you place your personal thoughts and concerns on your imaginary hook or in the safe, feel a sense of appreciation for your life, even with problems which you may be experiencing at the time. Appreciation of this kind can help to quiet the mind and get you into a baseball mind set.

3. Tell yourself that you will pick up your role as a person when you leave the clubhouse.

4. Focus on the process of getting ready to play and then competing, pitch by pitch.

PUT ON THE ROLE OF THE PERFORMER

Once you have mentally parked yourself as a person at the clubhouse door, what is it that you pick up?

What you should pick up and put on is your role of the performer. This is your first step in getting you ready for the day, whether that is a practice session or a game.

Putting on the role of a performer means getting yourself into the baseball mindset and role of being a baseball player. By doing this, you are willing to focus on this role to the exclusion of other things in your personal life.

Putting on the role of a performer involves being open and willing to the process of playing the game, given your role as a baseball performer and your position on the team.

The role of a baseball performer includes the following:

1. Following your pre game plan or routine so that you will be ready to compete.

2. Keeping your mind in the moment and on the task at hand, one pitch at a time.

3. Evaluating your performance accurately.

Here are some things to consider in assisting you in putting on the role of a baseball performer:

• Make sure that you have mentally parked yourself as a person at the clubhouse door.

• Make a commitment to your role as a baseball performer and focus on this.

• Know the specific things that you are being asked to do as a baseball player. These are the tasks that will help your team and to which you will contribute.

- Be ready to execute and to get the job done, one pitch at time, between the lines.

By focusing on your performance role, your role as a person is kept out of the performance equation.

BE MINDFUL OF THE MOMENT

Another useful way of keeping your self-esteem as a baseball player working for you, rather than against you, is to develop skill at keeping your mind in the moment.

When your mind is in the moment and on the immediate task at hand in the clubhouse and on the field, you are not influenced by your thoughts, concerns, and worries that cannot help you in those places.

Rather, you are paying attention to what matters with respect to your performance and what you are expected to do. In this regard, yourself and its consciousness recede to the background. You are more likely to maintain esteem for yourself, which is positive, since your mind is in the moment and not in the past or the future.

Being in the moment as a baseball player, though, requires that you learn to be mindful of the moment. This means being aware of what is going on now, as it is, as you observe it and not as you make judgments about it.

This awareness—mindfulness—occurs during a range of times— before, during, and after competition—as well as in different locations including the clubhouse, dugout, batter's box, and field.

Being mindful of the moment, and keeping your mind in the moment, can be developed by using the following guidelines.

1. Practice being aware. Make it a point when you are in the baseball setting to be mindful of the surroundings and the immediate task at hand. This is the case whether you are in the clubhouse, dugout, or during actual game situations. In being aware, you simply see what is there but do not judge it; you do not allow yourself as person to get involved. Rather, you just see, observe, and simply are aware of the moment without judgment. Try to deal with the task.

2. Watch out for the drift of your mind out of the present and into time periods and thoughts that are counterproductive to what you are doing to get ready to compete or to execute during the lines.

3. Whenever you observe that your mind is drifting and that you are starting to think of personal matters, just acknowledge this trend and just place your mind back into the moment.

KEEP SELF-JUDGMENT OUT OF YOUR PERFORMANCE

One of the greatest gifts that you have is your ability to make judgments about many things, including judgments about yourself. Self-judgments are good things to use for many aspects of your life. However, self-judgment can limit your performance and negatively affect your self-esteem as a baseball player—if used at incorrect times.

When you play the game of baseball, your focus needs to be on the task at hand and what you are expected to accomplish. When self-judgment is introduced into performance, however, you begin to pay attention to what you are saying and judging rather than focusing on the task at hand.

Consequently, you start to question what you are doing and why you are doing it.

When you can keep self-judgment out of your performance (that is, when you keep it separate from your performance) you get into a mode of observing what is happening but not making judgments. This will serve to maintain focus on the task at hand and foster positive self-esteem.

Here are some guidelines for keeping self-judgment out of your performance, while you are performing:

1. Mentally practice observing what you see as you perform and not make self-judgments about it. In this way, you keep the self out of the performance. For example, if the pitch you are throwing to the batter is outside and up, when it should have been inside and low, just observe that rather than make a judgment about it. ('The pitch should have been down. 'I am not sure why I can't get the ball down?")

2. As you compete, identify your tendency to judge, rather than observe. When you notice this tendency, step back and talk to yourself saying something like "observe don't judge" or some other word or phrase.

USE POSITIVE SELF-TALK

Your self-esteem as a baseball player also can be solidified through the use of positive self-talk. These are things which you affirm to yourself. In this regard, positive self-talk will keep you centered on who you are and what you have accomplished.

Positive self-talk can be used at any of the four levels of your development. Here are some examples:

- I am fortunate as a person, since I have a lovely family.

- I have been successful in weeding out the negatives from my life.

- I am fortunate to be part of a championship contending team.

- I have come a long way as a player from when I started out.

Positive self-talk is not aimed at fooling yourself. It is intended to remind you of what benefits you have and what you have accomplished. These kinds of statements—affirmations—allow you to feel positive but in a real way.

LOOK FOR THE "SMALL WINS"

Looking for the things that go well every day, not only in your baseball performance, but also in your life, can help maintain positive self-esteem.

Small wins are things like reading the sign correctly, pitching inside, staying composed, and other things.

When things are not going well for you on or off the baseball diamond, divide up the day into smaller segments, into an hour or even shorter time periods. Within each of those small time segments, look for what you have accomplished.

Looking for the small wins is a step by step approach. It enables you to seek the current picture and small things, not the big picture.

Looking for the small wins is especially helpful during times when things do not seem to be moving ahead and when you could tend to devalue yourself. Examples of these times are:

- During extended periods of physical rehabilitation

- When you are not performing well

- When you have been getting limited opportunities to play, either as a position player or as a relief pitcher

TAKE A PERSONAL INVENTORY

Being able to take stock of yourself is a very good way of helping to remain on an even personal keel. This is referred to as taking a personal inventory of yourself.

Within the baseball environment, nothing goes right or as expected all of the time, so it is good for your self-esteem to be able to put things in perspective. This can occur through a personal inventory.

Here are the steps to take for doing personal inventory.

1. Take a blank piece of paper.

2. On it, divide the paper in half. On one side, place the term, Person. On the other side, place the term, Performer.

3. Start with the Person side. In this area, list all of the good things that you have in your life including good things that are happening to you. Review these things and appreciate them. Save this information.

4. Now, take the performer side, List all the positives which have occurred for you as a baseball player. Do not get down on yourself in this task. Look for the small daily wins if need be. Consider all aspects of your game. Here too, review these positives and come to appreciate them. Save this information.

5. Periodically, when you may tend to get down on yourself, take out this inventory. Review it and appreciate what you have. Update it when something good or positive occurs that you want to remember and appreciate.

Table 14.1 is an example of a personal inventory which has been completed by a major league baseball player.

TABLE 14.1. Example of a personal inventory of a Major League baseball player

Person	Performer
• Family	• Talent
• Health	• Use my talent
• Enjoy life	• Like to compete
• Chance to help others	• Good career
• My faith	

WATCH OUT FOR THE BIG HEAD AND LITTLE HEAD

It is always important to watch out for signs that your self-esteem is out of kilter and that can steer you off course.

In this regard, there are two particular things that you can watch out for. These are;

1. The big head syndrome.

2. The little head syndrome.

The big head is when you start to think too much of yourself, especially as a performer. You tend to think that you are better than facts indicate. You anoint yourself with a big head. You start to inflate yourself.

When you start to recognize that you are getting a big head, step back, bring yourself back into the moment, and readjust back to being a good separator and being humble.

In contrast, look out for deflating of yourself. This is where you are so hard and demanding on yourself that you belittle yourself and give yourself a little head.

Here, too, step back, re-adjust, and get back into the moment; reviewing your personal inventory of positives can be used here (see previous guideline).

ENJOY THE PROCESS

Give your self-esteem a sure fire charger. This is committing to enjoying the process of playing the game. Condition yourself to making the process, active engagement in the game, as your primary outcome.

Reaffirm a commitment to playing the game for its own sake, over and above yourself.

EXERCISES

1.   Write a letter to your two selves—your personal side and then to your performer side. In the letter, give each side of yourself some advice about how it can stay on an even keel, without having to rely on the other side.

2.   Identify the red flag situations when you tend to get caught up in your performance and do yourself in. For each of these situations, make note of how you can deal with them and prevent them from occurring.

3.   If you were unable to play baseball anymore, starting right now, how would you feel and what would be your plan for life without baseball?

CHAPTER FIFTEEN

———— ⟡ ————

PERFORMANCE ACCOUNTABILITY: TAKING RESPONSIBILITY FOR YOUR RESULTS

Performance accountability is the eleventh domain of the Complete Mental Game. It is an area that is very important to your day to day and longer range performance. It involves taking responsibility for your results and using feedback about them to make adjustments and to get better.

Performance accountability is a responsibility, however, that can easily be neglected. This is the case, especially when you are playing a string of games, night after night. During those times, with one game coming after another, it is easy to not take the time to review your performance.

In addition, there are some natural human tendencies to stay away from reviewing your performance.

For one, when a player is performing well, he is likely to continue doing what he has been doing. However, he may not have taken the time or used an approach to understand why this success is happening for him.

In contrast, when things are not going as well on the field, there can be a tendency of the player to deny things and to not evaluate his results.

Being accountable for performance is a hallmark of a solid baseball player, a true professional.

This kind of player does not leave things to chance. He realizes that some things are under his control, while other things are not. This player wants to take responsibility to understand and act on the things that are under his control.

QUALITIES OF THE ACCOUNTABLE PLAYER

The baseball player can only be accountable for things over which he has influence and control. These are the things which he should be accountable for and seek to understand.

There are five qualities that are present in a player who is skilled in the domain of performance accountability. These qualities are the following:

1. The player wants to be responsible for his game performances as well as for his overall development as a baseball player.

2. He is ready to be accountable for how he has done on the baseball diamond, rather than waiting for a coach or an instructor to come to him about his performance.

3. He is willing to face the facts about his performance, no matter how poor or mediocre they may be. In this respect, the player desires to be an accurate evaluator of his performance. He does not want to cheat himself or others, especially his teammates. He is strong enough to not make excuses or to turn his head and deny things.

4. The player has a systematic approach where he reviews his performance and evaluates it accurately. This approach becomes part of the player's overall process.

5. He uses the resulting information about his performance to make adjustments in the various parts of his game, not only over the short term but also during the longer haul of the season.

ADVANTAGES OF BEING ACCOUNTABLE FOR YOUR PERFORMANCE

There are several advantages to you as a baseball player for being ready, willing and able to be accountable for your game performances and for your overall development as a baseball player. These advantages are the following;

1. Since you are motivated to be an accurate self-evaluator, you are able to gather useful information about your performance—what you have done well or not so well in the game. With this information, you can learn more about yourself, make adjustments, and improve your performance.

2. You develop a feeling of confidence and control about the process of playing the game since you have committed to a systematic approach.

3. You create the opportunity for yourself to master valuable skills—accurate self-evaluation—that can be transferred to other aspects of your life such as school, family life, or business.

4. You make a statement about not leaving important things to chance, since you are accountable about your performance and accurate in your assessment of it.

DISADVANTAGES OF NOT BEING ACCOUNTABLE FOR YOUR PERFORMANCE

If someone chooses to not be accountable for their performance, there are some negatives that can come with that kind of attitude. These disadvantages are the following;

1. When you are not accountable for your performance, you run the risk of using limited or incomplete information about how you performed and also what controllable factors may have been responsible for it.

2. You can easily develop an uncomfortable feeling of not knowing what to do next, particularly if things are not going well on the field.

3. You may feel like things are spinning out of control in terms of your game.

GUIDELINES FOR PERFORMANCE ACCOUNTABILITY

In order to be responsible for your results as a baseball player and therefore be accountable to yourself, there are several guidelines which can be offered. These guidelines are the following;

1. Identify your controllables

2. Review the videotape

3. Conduct a plus/minus meeting with yourself

4. Discuss your performance

5. Learn from your performance

6. Detect accurate self-evaluation problems

7. Use a player journal

IDENTIFY YOUR CONTROLLABLES

If you want to be successful at being a consistent baseball performer, one who contributes to the team and to winning games, center your attention on the things which you can control.

It makes no sense to deal with things which are beyond your control—umpiring, weather, fans, etc.—since these factors will not do you or your game any good, if you pay attention to them.

Your controllables are the parts of your game which you can influence and on which you should center your time, energy, and performance accountability efforts.

Your controllables as a baseball player encompass many things. Here are a few examples:

1. How you use your thoughts, emotions, and actions, both on and off the baseball diamond.

2. How you prepare for each game—getting ready to compete.

3. How you keep yourself focused on and engaged in the game.

4. How you approach and take your at bats in terms of things like having a plan, plate discipline, and proper swing mechanics.

5. How you implement your pitching plan for each game and how you make adjustments to it as the game proceeds.

6. How you field your position.

As you set out to review and evaluate your game performance, make sure that you are looking at the things which are under your control. When you look for the things that are under your control, you are able to specify what they are—name them—and then take ownership of them—claim them.

REVIEW THE VIDEOTAPE

The review of videotape of your game performance can be helpful as part of being accountable for your performance.

In order to review videotape about your performance, however, the following conditions need to be present:

1. The video of your performance needs to be clear, and which allows you to study your performance.

2. The video needs to be captured which depicts important aspects of your performance such as your at bats, or the quality of your pitches during the outing.

3. You need to have someone you trust who can get the video to you in time for you to review it the day after the game.

When you do review video about your performance, however, use these steps:

1. Make sure that you have access to the hardware to review the footage such as a video recorder or your lap top.

2. Set aside a specific time for looking at the tape, with focus and purpose.

3. Decide if you want to watch the video alone or with your coach. You may want to watch it alone first and then discuss it with your coach at another scheduled time.

4. Observe what you see on the tape, and its meaning. For instance, did it show things you did well (your pluses) or aspects of your performance which were not that good (your minuses). Then, challenge yourself on why you performed that way: why you did well, or why you did not do so well.

5. Concentrate on being a good observer of your performance as well as an accurate self-evaluator. Do not look the other way. Be honest, no matter what the results.

6. Get ready to review what you have found with yourself and your coaches.

7. Use the information to develop your approach to playing the game, given your position.

Conduct a Plus/Minus Meeting with Yourself

One of the ways to be accountable for your game performance is having a meeting with yourself. This is referred to as a plus/minus meeting.

A plus/minus meeting is a systematic way of reviewing and evaluating your performance in a particular game.

The purpose of the meeting is to review the things you did well in the game and the things that you did not do so well, and then use that information to make adjustments to your game.

A plus/minus meeting is best conducted the day after the game, rather than immediately following it which often is an emotional time.

However, whenever you review your performance, make sure that your mind is clear and that your emotions are on an even keel.

Figure 15.1: Plus/Minus Review Form

Plus/Minus Review Form

Name: _____ Position: _____ Date: _____

Pluses for the Game (Physical, Mental, Fundamental)	Minuses for the Game (Physical, Mental, Fundamental
1.	1.
2.	2.
3.	3.
4.	4.
5.	5.

Here are the steps that you can use to conduct a plus/minus meeting with yourself for reviewing your performance:

1. Draw a line down the middle of a piece of paper, thereby dividing the paper into two halves. On one half of the paper, label "Pluses", and then label "Minuses" on the other half. You also can use a copy of the plus/minus form, an example of which is seen Figure 15.1.

2. Think about your last game, the one in which you most recently competed. Identify the things that are under your control and which you did especially well during the game. Consider all areas of that game and how you performed— mental, fundamental, and physical. List these as your pluses. Three or four pluses will be sufficient, if you can come up with that many.

3. For each of your pluses, ask yourself this question: Why was this a plus for me? Make sure you understand the why, the reason why it happened. You may even want to write the why, or the reason, down.

4. Now, go to the minus side from that game. Identify the

things that you did not do well during the game and which also are under your control. Here too, three or four minuses will be sufficient, if you have that many.

5. For each of the minuses, ask the same questions which you did with the pluses: Why are these minuses? Make sure that you understand the reasons which you give.

6. You can use this information as a basis for discussion with your coach, or you can use it for improving your game.

Figure 15.2 is an example of information from a plus/minus meeting which a major league starting pitcher used to review one of his outings.

Figure 15.2: Example of a completed Plus/Minus Review Form

Plus/Minus Review Form

Name: Major League Pitcher   Position: xxxxxxxxxxxxxx   Date: xxxxxx

Pluses for the Game (Physical, Mental, Fundamental)	Minuses for the Game (Physical, Mental, Fundamental)
1. Kept command of my fastball	1. Reluctant to use changeup
2. Good rhythm and tempo	2. Distracted by rain and field conditions
3. Got swings & misses	3.
4. Good bullpen	4.
5.	5.

DISCUSS YOUR PERFORMANCE

As part of being accountable for your results, you can meet with your coach to discuss your performance.

This meeting with your coach will allow you to compare your own version of your performance with what the other individual thinks about it.

In addition, discussing your performance will allow you to get a read on the similarities and differences of your pluses and minuses with the other individual.

Here are some steps to consider in discussing your performance with your coach:

1. Set up a specific time to meet with your manager or coach.

2. Be prepared to discuss the performance of your most recent game, based on your review if it. This can be the information which you derived from a plus/minus meeting with yourself.

3. Listen to what your coach has to say. If there are differences of opinion between you and the coach, discuss it and work to get resolution on the differences.

4. Request from your coach his opinions about what you need to do for your next game or outing.

5. Ask the coach what he learned about you from this most recent performance.

6. Use the information from this discussion to help you improve your development or enhance your performance.

LEARN FROM YOUR PERFORMANCE

The basic reason for conducting a review of your performance is to learn from it and to use the information for upcoming games—to fix it and to apply it.

In order to make this happen, here are some things to consider:

1. Make sure that you have pinpointed your pluses and minuses from the game. Without this specific information, you cannot learn anything, other than generalities.

2. For your pluses and for your minuses, understand why each one of them is a plus or a minus. Knowing the reason behind the plus or the minus will provide you with the information you need to know.

3. Given the information which you have gained , consider the following questions;

- What do I need to keep doing that has been successful?

- What changes do I need to make in order to be successful?

- How am I going to make this adjustment?

- Who else should know this?

DETECT ACCURATE SELF-EVALUATION PROBLEMS

As you proceed to review and evaluate your game performances, make sure to monitor yourself on situations when you may be less than honest with yourself. In this regard, detect accurate self-evaluation problems. Here are several red flag situations:

1. Not being honest with yourself about the facts, realities, and results of your game performance.

2. Not being specific enough about what you did well and what you did not do so well.

3. Not asking why—that is, the reasons for your pluses and minuses

4. Not using what you have learned from your review to make adjustments.

USE A PLAYER JOURNAL

A player journal is a tool that you can use to monitor your performance, especially over the course of the season.

There is no one best format to maintain a journal. The journal could be a notebook, a three ring binder, or kept in your laptop computer.

Here is information which can be kept as part of a player journal that can promote your accountability for your performance:

1. A section where you keep copies of your plus/minus meetings.

2. Comments about how you felt about each game.

3. Notes about how you performed against other teams or against opposing pitchers or hitters.

4. Other information about your performance that has meaning for you.

EXERCISES

1. Identify your success factors. These are the controllables which are most important for your successful game performance. Write down why each one is important. Use this information as the basis for monitoring and reviewing your performance.

2. Try to locate one or more players whom you know who use a player journal. Discuss how they use the journal. This is likely to give you ideas about how you can use one for yourself.

3. How have you used videotape to evaluate your performance? What have been the advantages and limitations of using videotape? How can you best proceed in incorporating videotape as part of the review of your performance?

CHAPTER SIXTEEN

───────── ⚾ ─────────

CONTINUOUS IMPROVEMENT: STRIVING TO GET BETTER

Continuous improvement is the twelfth domain of the Complete Mental Game. It reflects a developmental and forward looking approach which you have about yourself, as a baseball player and as a person, both on and off the baseball diamond.

Continuous improvement reflects making adjustments and striving to get better with your game, baseball career, and overall life.

Continuous improvement involves agreeing with yourself to "never say never" about your development not only as a baseball player but also as a person.

In the Japanese culture, the word, "kaizen" means continuous improvement in that an individual is striving to always get better in business and other areas such as family life and education.

In terms of the Complete Mental Game, continuous improvement challenges you to be the best that you can be and to continue to take this approach as you proceed in baseball and life.

PERSONAL COMMITMENTS TO YOUR CONTINUOUS IMPROVEMENT

Continuous improvement requires that you make some very important personal commitments. These commitments provide you with the respect and care that you deserve. You are in charge of these commitments.

These are three personal commitments which can help you place things in perspective and to make sure that you are moving in positive directions for you and for those who are part of your support system.

COMMITMENT I: BEING THE BEST I CAN BE

This commitment is for you to decide to be the best that you can be—as a player and as a person—on and off the baseball diamond. This commitment to your continuous improvement challenges you to ask and answer these questions:

> *Am I striving to be the best that I can be, each and every day? If so, how committed am I? If not, why not?*

COMMITMENT II: ACCURATE SELF EVALUATION

This commitment is making sure that you have a way of evaluating your progress as a player and as person. The task here is to take inventory of yourself in terms of all of the other eleven mental domains that already have been discussed in other chapters of this book. In particular, some things to monitor about yourself are how you are doing in keeping up to date on your core values, knowing your strong points and limitations, setting and pursuing goals, staying on an even personal keel, and taking responsibility for your results. Here the questions to ask yourself are the following:

> *Am I evaluating my progress in baseball and life, honestly? If so, how committed am I to accurate self-evaluation? If not, why not?*

COMMITMENT III: PERSONAL PLAN

This commitment is to create a plan for your life once your baseball playing days have been completed. The best questions to ask yourself in relation to this commitment are the following:

> *What is my current plan for baseball and what is my plan for my life? If I do not have a plan, why not?*

Advantages of Being Committed to Your Continuous Improvement

There are many advantages for you if you make a commitment to continually improve yourself as a baseball player and as a person. Three main advantages are the following:

1. Since you are always striving to get better, you will not become stagnant or complacent. This is because you will be honest and realistic in terms of yourself and your overall development. You will always be seeking new tasks to accomplish and challenges to take on.

2. Since you will be seeking new things, and trying to improve yourself, you will most likely enjoy the process of playing the game and leading a life which is important to you.

3. You are likely to maintain momentum in moving in positive directions, once your playing days have been completed.

Disadvantages of Not Being Committed to Your Continuous Improvement

However, if you do not commit to your continuous improvement, you can put yourself at a distinct disadvantage. Some disadvantages are the following:

1. You can develop a false sense of security. In this sense, you can get into a state where you delude yourself that everything will remain the same for you as a baseball player and even as a person.

2. You will not be honest and realistic about yourself. In this regard, you may attempt to deceive yourself about where you are in the game.

3. You will limit the opportunities that can be available to you once you are no longer able to play baseball, since you have not considered them in a systematic way.

Guidelines for Continuous Improvement

In order to assist you in making a commitment to your continuous improvement, there are some guidelines provided in the remainder of this chapter, for your consideration. These guidelines are the following:

1. Pinpoint What You Want to Learn

2. Decide How You Learn

3. Create a Plan for Your Learning

4. Conduct a Personal Inventory

5. Be in Charge of Your Transition from the Game

Pinpoint What You Want to Learn

Do yourself a favor and learn about what you want to learn and get better at.

Continuous improvement involves learning—lifelong learning—in many areas that include education, family, finances, baseball, and other areas.

So, make sure that you know what constitutes learning for you and what are the most important areas in which you need to continue to improve.

In this way, you can also be at the top of your game in the learning category and continually improve.

Learning involves changes in your knowledge, skills and abilities, based on experience. So, make it a point to pinpoint what you want to learn.

In this regard, pinpoint what you want to learn about the following areas:

1. *Baseball*: This may involve learning about adjustments which you need to make in your game or with your career.

2. *Family*: This may include some new things that you need to learn more about such as being a good parent, or communication with your spouse.

3. *Education*: This may include courses which you need to take so that you can successfully complete your degree.

4. *Business*: This may include learning about business opportunities that you can take once your career is over.

5. *Community*: This may include learning about how to establish a charitable foundation.

6. *Physical*: This may include learning how to lower your cholesterol.

7. *Recreational*: This may include learning how to play a new sport for recreational purposes.

8. *Spiritual*: This may include learning how to become more aware of the spiritual dimensions as part of your life.

9. *Other*: other things which are relevant to you.

DECIDE HOW YOU LEARN

Once you have identified what you want to learn more about, decide how you are going to learn these things. To do this you need to ask yourself how you learn best.

In this regard, there are three basic ways to learn. These three ways of learning go by the acronym, VAK. VAK stands for three learning modalities:

Visual: This is learning by seeing such as observing another person, watching a video tape or observing someone else, live.

Auditory: This is learning by listening such as by discussing what you want to learn with someone who is experienced.

Kinesthetic: This is learning by doing such as practicing the physical skills that you want to learn.

Now, determine which of the above three modalities has been

your preferred way or ways of learning. At this point, ask yourself the following questions:

1. What is my most preferred way of learning something new? Is this visual, auditory, or learning by doing?

2. When I need to learn something, what are my greatest obstacles?

3. When I want to learn something, how do I get myself ready to learn?

4. What do I want to learn at this time which will make me a better baseball player? A better person?

CREATE A PLAN FOR YOUR LEARNING

Whenever you want to accomplish something—in baseball and beyond—you can improve your chances by having a plan. This also applies to your learning and your continuous improvement.

Once you have decided what you want to learn and how, you can put that information into a learning plan.

This task is similar in format and process to a game plan or a plan for your at bats. It involves specifying the following information:

1. Area—this is the area of learning such as education, business, family etc.

2. Goals—this is what you want to learn

3. Activities—this is how you are going to learn (attain the goals)

4. Evaluation—this is how you are going to decide how much you are learning

Table 16. 1 is an example of a learning plan for a veteran major league baseball player who was at the end of his baseball career.

TABLE 16.1. Example of a learning plan for a veteran Major League player.

Goal	Activities
Decide my next steps in life, following retirement	• Learn what it takes to be a minor league coach – ask coaches, former coaches • Investigate online law school programs for possible application for admission in two years. • Improve public speaking skills.

CONDUCT A PERSONAL INVENTORY

As you proceed in your baseball career, take a personal inventory. This is a way of deciding where you are now in various areas of baseball and life.

You then can use the information from the personal inventory to make adjustments to your situations.

Then, you will be able to decide what you can do next to make adjustments so that you can continue to strive to be the best that you can be.

Here is a personal inventory of items that you can use. In doing so, you can use this rating scale for each item.

- Yes
- No
- Not Sure

1. At present, baseball is effectively balanced with the other important parts of my life.

2. I have a good understanding of my current strong points and limitations as a baseball player.

3. I have a good understanding of my strong points and limitations as a person.

4. I want to continue to play baseball at this point in time.

5. I want to continue my education at this point in time.

6. Presently, I am confident in my abilities to continue with my baseball career.

7. Right now, I am confident in my abilities to succeed outside of the game.

8. I have a plan for my continued development in baseball.

9. I have a plan for my continued development outside of the game.

10. I want to be able to contribute to and give back to my community.

11. Once I retire as a player from baseball, I want to continue to be involved in the game.

12. I have available to me, specific people with whom I can share my personal and professional concerns.

13. My financial situation is in order.

14. I want to establish a charitable foundation.

15. Once my career is over, I want to stay out of the game.

For each item of the inventory in which you have answered, "Yes", make sure that you have been accurate in your self-evaluation and that you have plan for following through.

For each item of the inventory in which you have answered, "No", make sure that have a way of deciding what you may need to do next.

For any item for which you have responded, "Not Sure", attempt to seek out people or information which will turn your response into a "Yes" or a "No".

BE IN CHARGE OF YOUR TRANSITION FROM THE GAME

Playing the game of baseball will not last forever for you and for everyone else. Unfortunately, there are players who do not recognize this reality or who tend to deny it.

The task of transitioning out of the game of baseball is something that should not be neglected or left to chance. It is an area which can be under your personal control and influence, if you want to accept the challenge.

When it is time for you to consider leaving the game or retiring from it, here are questions which you should ask yourself:

1. Why do I want to stop playing baseball?

2. What are my immediate options for life outside of baseball?

3. Do I want to continue my education?

4. What is my current financial situation?

5. How am I going to make my transition successful? What people, procedures, and places can I rely on?

6. What would happen if baseball ended for me today?

Exercises

1. What have I learned to date in my baseball career that has already made me a better player? Consider all areas in the physical, mental, and fundamental domains.

2. What is my plan for the coming year: Baseball? Life?

3. What are the biggest obstacles to my continuous improvement and how can I overcome these obstacles?

4. What are books, videos, and other resources that I want to review that may help me with my continuous improvement?

ABOUT THE AUTHOR

Dr. Charlie Maher is Sport Psychologist and Director of Psychological Services for the Cleveland Indians of Major League Baseball (MLB). He has been part of the organization since 1995. In addition, Dr. Maher is the sport psychologist for the Cleveland Browns (NFL), Cleveland Cavaliers (NBA), and Minnesota Wild (NHL). Dr. Maher is also a Full Professor of Psychology at the Graduate School of Applied and Professional Psychology, Rutgers University. For 25 years, Dr. Maher has provided sport and performance psychology services for individuals, teams, and organizations in baseball, basketball, football, hockey, tennis, horse racing, boxing, and other sports as well as in business, military, and educational settings.

APPENDIX A:

THE COMPLETE MENTAL GAME OF BASEBALL CHECKLIST

THE COMPLETE MENTAL GAME
OF BASEBALL CHECKLIST

Dr. Charlie Maher

Complete this checklist to review your Compete Mental Game. Rate yourself on each area, using this scale: 3= I am above average in the area; 2= I am average in this area; 1= I am below average in this area. Use your ratings to get better.

I. *QUALITY PREPARATION--- Am I Prepared to Compete?*

___1. **Perspective**: I keep baseball balanced with the rest of my life

___2. **Personal Awareness**: I understand my current strong points and limitations, on and off the baseball diamond.

___3. **Self-Motivation**: I enthusiastically pursue baseball related goals that are specific, measurable, attainable, relevant and time-framed.

___4. **Mental Discipline:** I have a plan for my development and follow through with it.

II. *COMPETITIVE FOLLOW THROUGH--- Is My Mind in the Moment?*

___5. **Self-Confidence**: I believe that I possess the capacity to compete, pitch by pitch, play by play, inning by inning.

___6. **Emotional Intensity:** I compete with effective energy and effort, as the game begins and throughout the contest.

___7. **Focus:** I am able to keep my mind in the moment and on the task at hand, one pitch at a time, both sides of the plate.

___8. **Composure:** I remain poised and under emotional control, especially during pressure game situations.

____9. **Teamwork**: I relate productively and respectfully with teammates, coaches, and others.

III. *ACCURATE SELF-EVALUATION--- Am I Honest about My Results?*

____10.**Self-Esteem:** I keep myself as a person separate from myself as a baseball player, no matter how I perform, good or not so good.

____11.**Performance Accountability**: I take responsibility for my performance and make necessary adjustments as a hitter, pitcher, fielder or other areas.

____12. **Continuous Improvement**: I strive to get better as a person and performer, day by day, both in season and during the off season.

References

The content of this book is based on my experiences as a sport psychologist in professional baseball and in other sports, as well as my research and evaluation activities in those areas. In addition, the theories and empirical research contained in the following sources also have helped to shape this book and the instructional system described in it.

Aldwin, C.M. *Stress, Coping and Development: An Integrative Perspective.* New York: Guilford Press, 1994.

Bass, B. *Leadership and Performance beyond Expectations.* New York: Free Press, 1985.

Baumeister, R.E. "Choking under Pressure: Self Consciousness and Paradoxical Effects of Incentives on Skilled Performance." *Journal of Personality and Social Psychology* 46 (1984): 610-620.

Beilock, S. *Choke: What the Secrets of the Brain Reveal about Getting it Right When You Have To.* New York: Free Press, 2010.

Beilock, S.L. and R. Gray. "Why Do Athletes Choke under Pressure?" In *Handbook of Sport Psychology,* edited by Gershon Tenenbaum and Robert C. Eklund, 425-444. New York: Wiley, 2007.

Bernier, M. and others. "Mindfulness and Acceptance Approaches in

Sport Performance." *Journal of Clinical Sport Psychology* 3 (2009): 320-333.

Cattell, H. and J. Schuerger. *Essentials of 16PF Assessment.* Hoboken, NJ: John Wiley & Sons, 2003.

Colvin, G. *Talent is Overrated: What Really Separates World-Class Performers from Everybody Else.* New York: Portfolio, 2009.

Deci, E.L. and R.U. Ryan. *Intrinsic Motivation and Self-Determination in Human Behavior.* New York: Plenum Press, 1985.

Duncan, S. *Present Moment Awareness.* San Diego, CA: Present Moment Thought, 2001.

Gallwey, W. Timothy. *The Inner Game of Tennis: The Classic Guide to the Mental Side of Peak Performing.* New York: Random House, 2008.

Gardner, F.L. and Z.E. Moore. *Clinical Sport Psychology.* Champaign, IL: Human Kinetics, 2006.

Gardner, F.L. and Z.E. Moore. *The Psychology of Human Performance: The Mindfulness-Acceptance-Commitment Approach.* New York: Springer Publishing Company, 2009.

Gilbert, D. *Stumbling on Happiness.* New York: Vintage, 2005.

Goleman, D. *Emotional Intelligence.* New York: Bantam Books, 1995.

Hackman, J.R. *Groups that Work.* San Francisco, CA: Jossey-Bass, 1990.

Hanin, Y. "Emotions in Sport: Current Issues and Perspectives." In *Handbook of Sport Psychology*, edited by Gershon Tenenbaum and Robert C. Eklund, 425-444. New York: Wiley, 2007.

Hanin Y., ed. *Emotions in Sport.* Champaign, IL: Human Kinetics, 2000.

Hahn, T.N. *The Miracle of Mindfulness*. Boston: Beacon, 1976.

Hayes, S.C., K.D. Strosohl, and K. Wilson. *Acceptance and Commitment Therapy: An Experiential Approach to Behavior Change*. New York: Guilford Press, 1999.

Hodges, N.J., J.L. Stankers, and C. MacMahon. "Expert Performance in Sport: A Cognitive Perspective." In *The Cambridge Handbook of Expertise and Expert Performance*, edited by K. Anders Erricson, N. Channess, P.J. Feltovich, and R.R. Hoffman, 471-488. New York: Cambridge University Press, 2006.

Kabot-Zin, J. *Coming to Our Senses: Healing Ourselves and the World through Mindfulness*. New York: Hyperion, 2005.

Koch, R. *The 80/20 Principle: The Secret to Achieving More with Less*. New York: Doubleday, 1998.

Lazarus, R.S. *Emotion and Adaptation*. New York: Oxford University Press, 1981.

Lazarus, R.S. and S. Folkman. *Stress, Appraisal, and Coping*. New York: Springer, 1981.

Lazarus, R.S. "Cognitive-Motivational-Relational Theory of Emotion." In *Emotions in Sport*, edited by Y. Hanin. Champaign, IL: Human Kinetics, 2000.

Lehrer, J. *How We Decide*. New York: Houghton Mifflin, 2009.

McMannis, T. *Acquisition and Performance of Sport Skills*. Chichester, West Sussex, England: Psychology Press, 2004.

Millman, D. *Body, Mind and Mastery: Creating Success in Sport and Life*. Novato, CA: New World Library, 1999.

Oliver, J.D. and P. Chodren. *Commit to Sit: Tools for Cultivating a Meditation Practice*. New York: Hay House, 2009.

Peterson, C. and M. Seligman. *Character Strengths and Virtues: A Handbook and Classification*. New York: Oxford University Press, 2004.

Pinker, S. *The Stuff of Thought: Language Differences as a Window into Human Nature*. New York: Viking, 2007.

Salmon, Paul and others. *Human Factors Methods and Sports Science: A Practical Guide*. New York: CRC Press, 2009.

Stadler, M. *The Psychology of Baseball*. New York: Gotham Books, 2007.

Vallerand, R.J. "Intrinsic and Extrinsic Motivation in Sport and Physical Activity: A Review and a Look at the Future." In *Handbook of Sport Psychology*, edited by Gershon Tenenbaum and Robert C. Eklund, 59-83. New York: Wiley, 2007.

Vealy, R. "Mental Skills Training in Sport." In *Handbook of Sport Psychology*, edited by Gershon Tenenbaum and Robert C. Eklund, 287-309. New York: Wiley, 2007.

Vickers, J. *Perception, Cognition, and Decision Training*. Champaign, IL: Human Kinetics, 2007.

Ward, P.A., A. Williams, and P.A. Hancock. "Simulation for Performance and Training." In *The Cambridge Handbook of Expertise and Expert Performance*, edited by K. Anders Erricson, N. Channess, P.J. Feltovich, and R.R. Hoffman, 243-262. New York: Cambridge University Press, 2006.

Williams, J.M., ed. *Applied Sport Psychology: Personal Growth to Peak Performance*, 5th ed. Boston: McGraw-Hill, 2006.